THIS BOOK BELONGS TO:

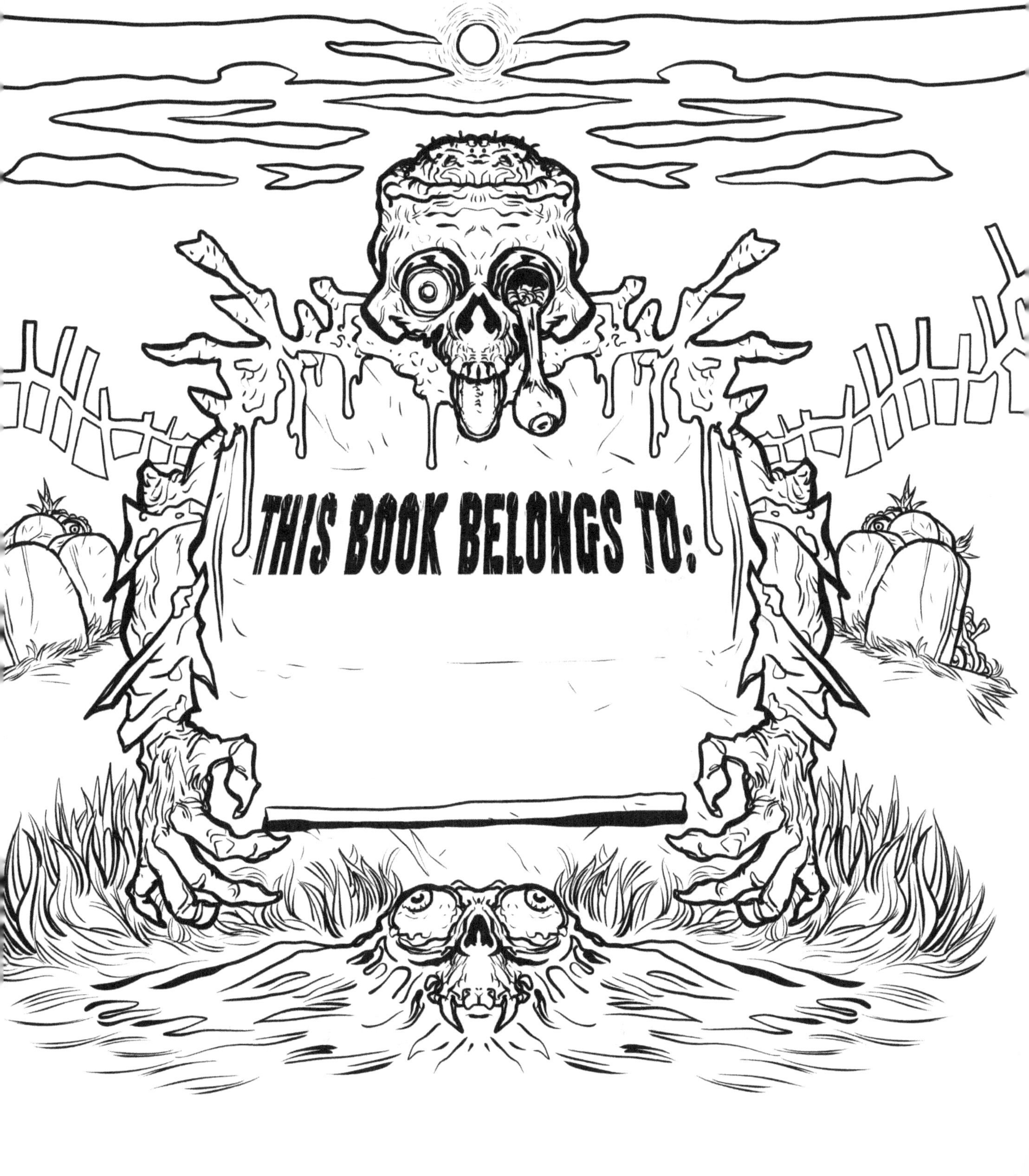

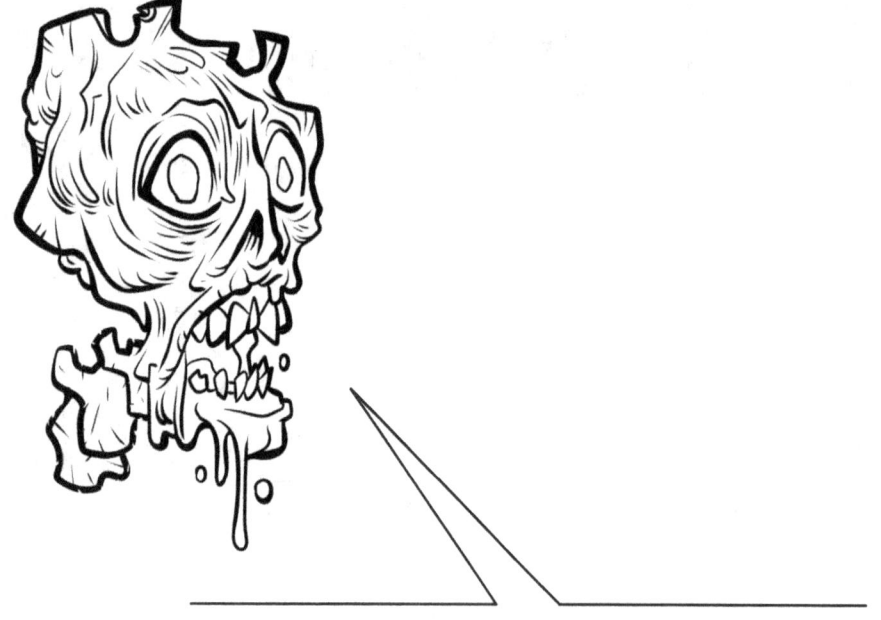

A GORACLE OF THINGS TO COME.

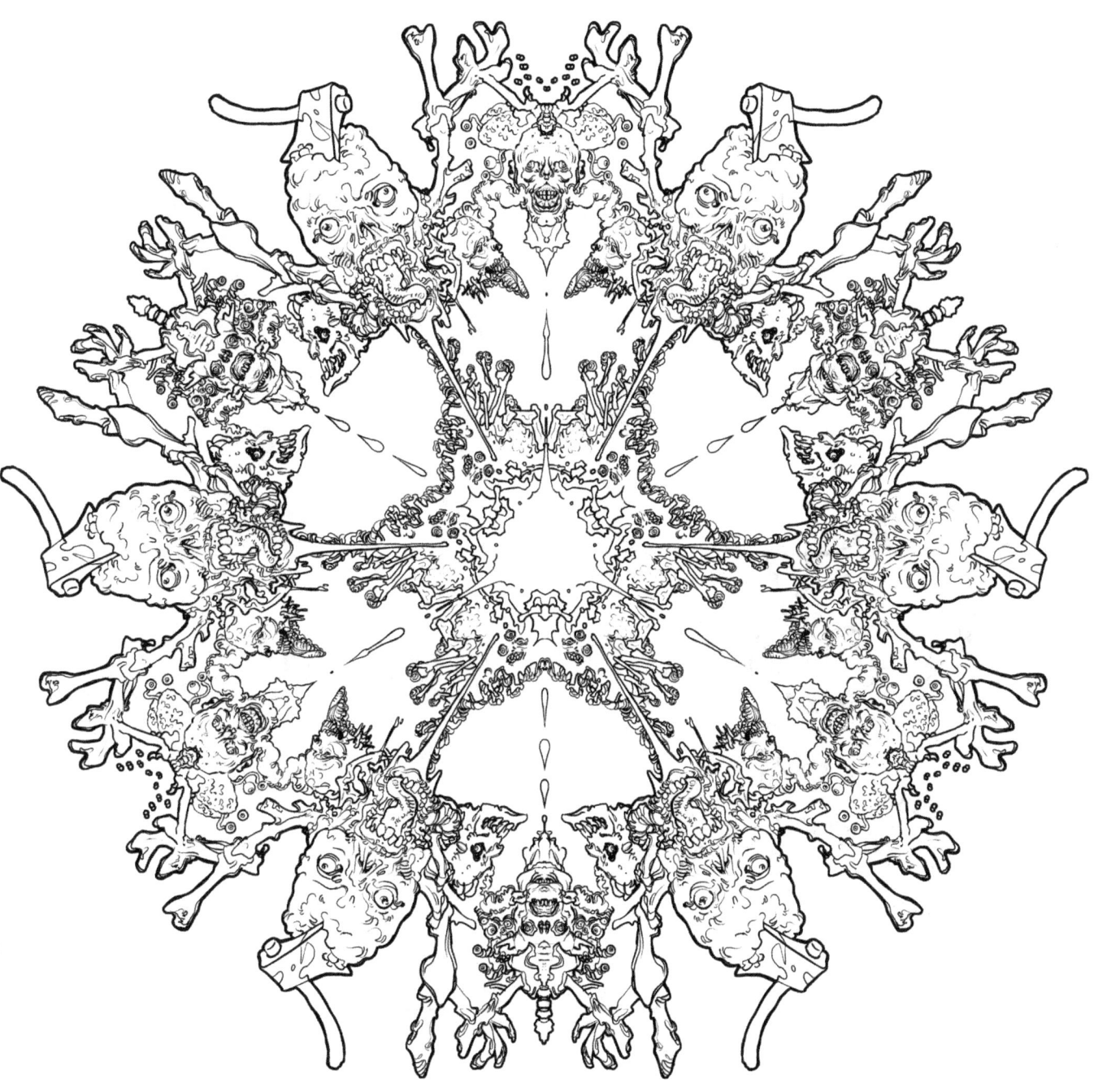

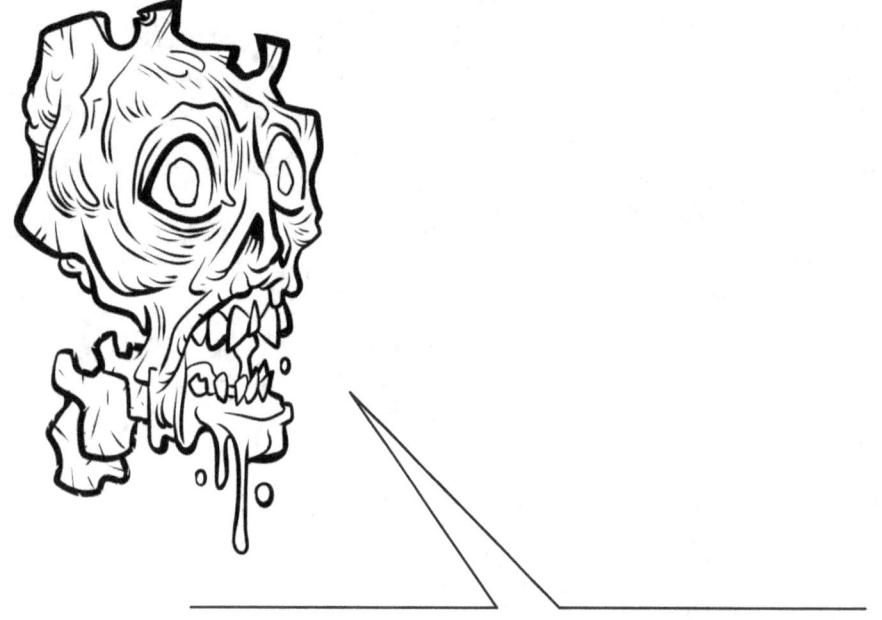

A DERAILED INHUMAN.

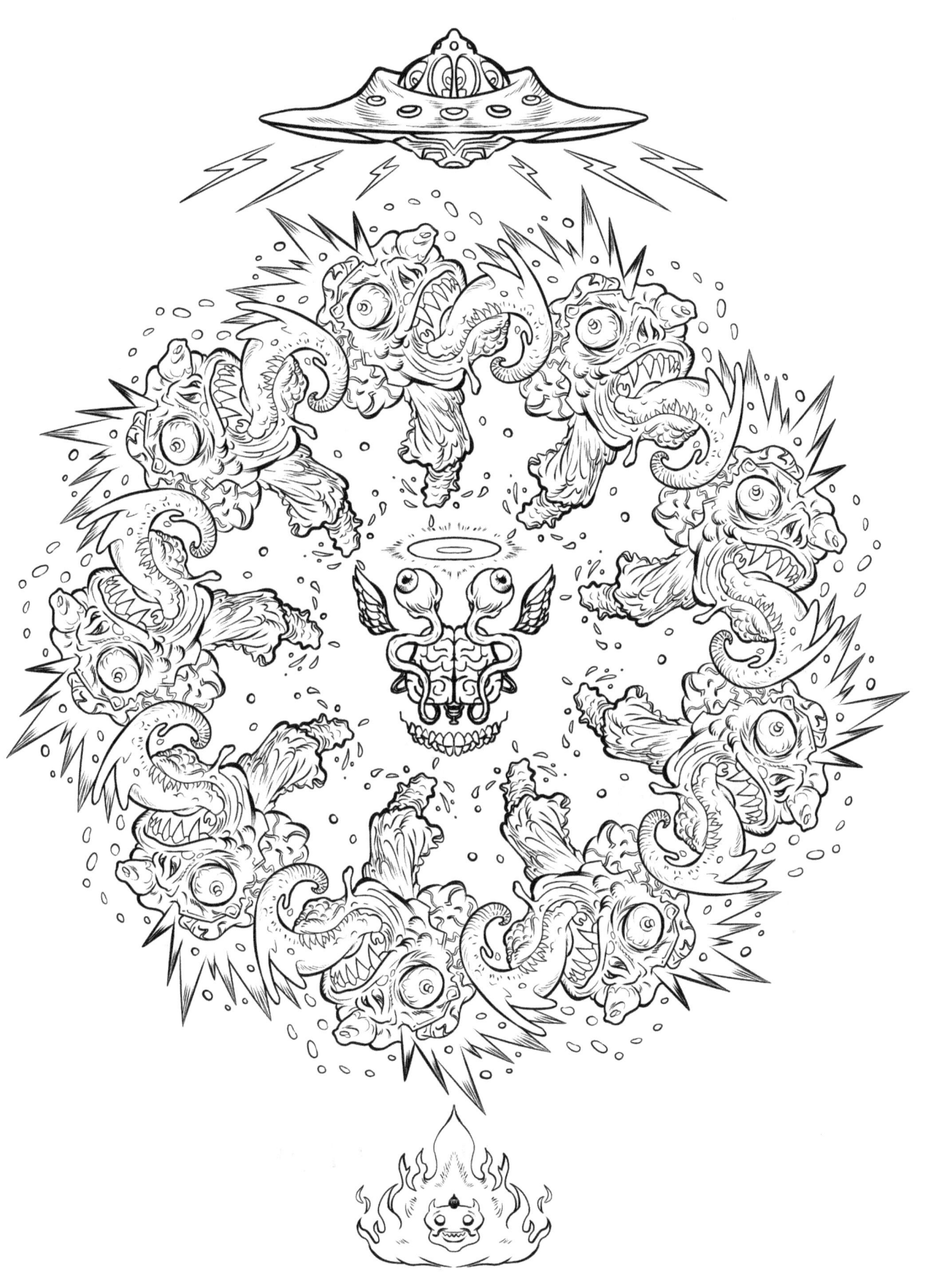

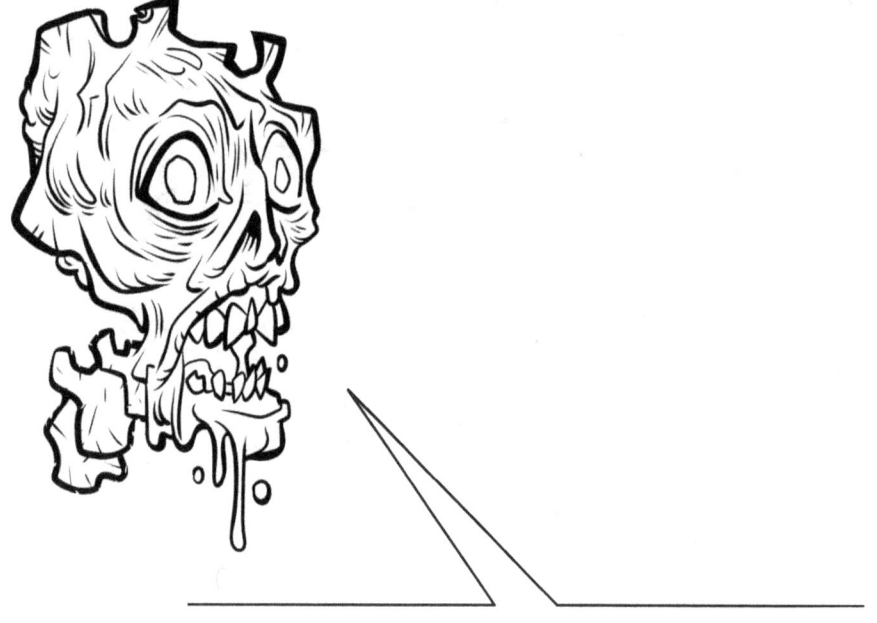

A FRIGHTFUL TRIAD.

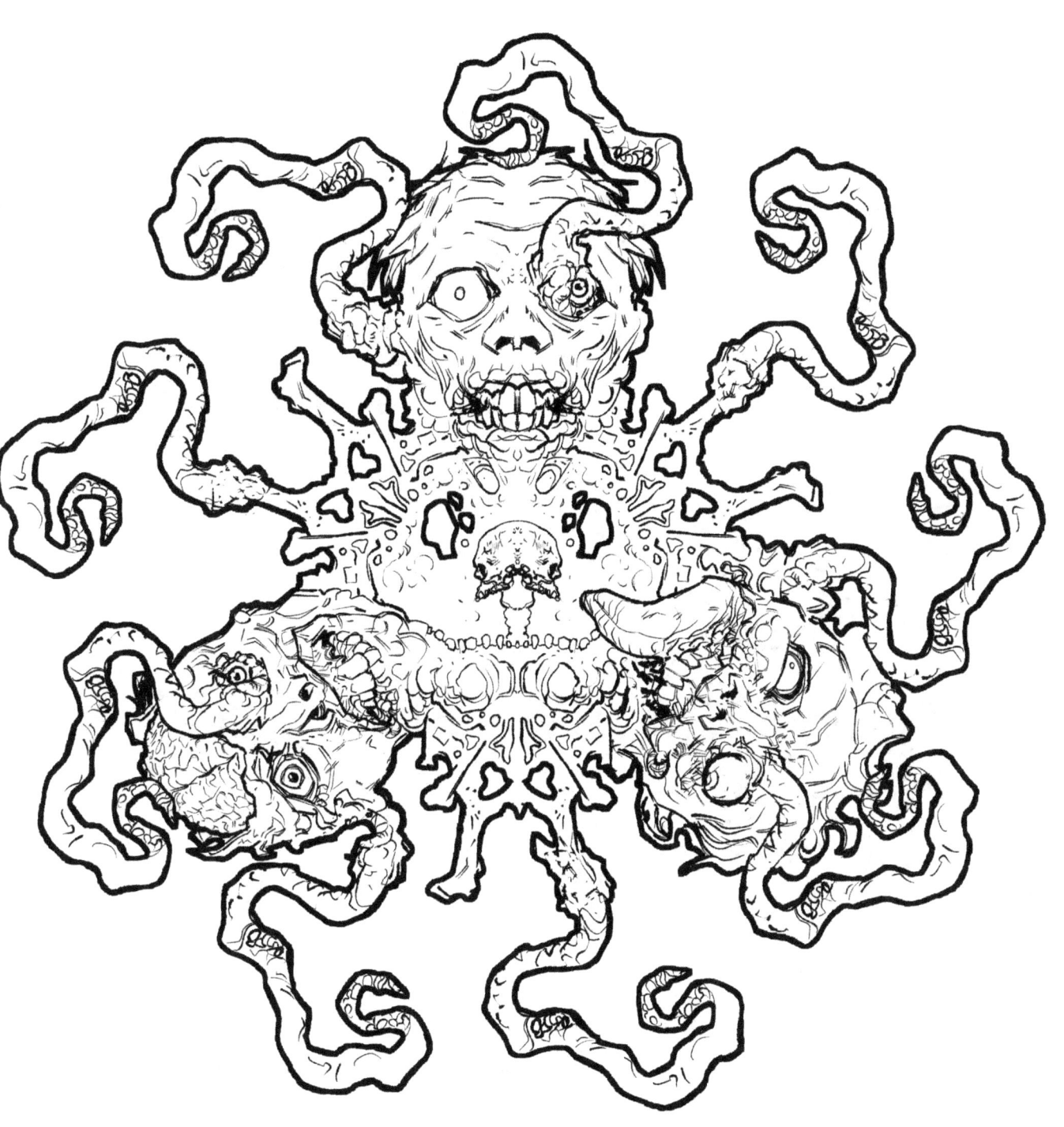

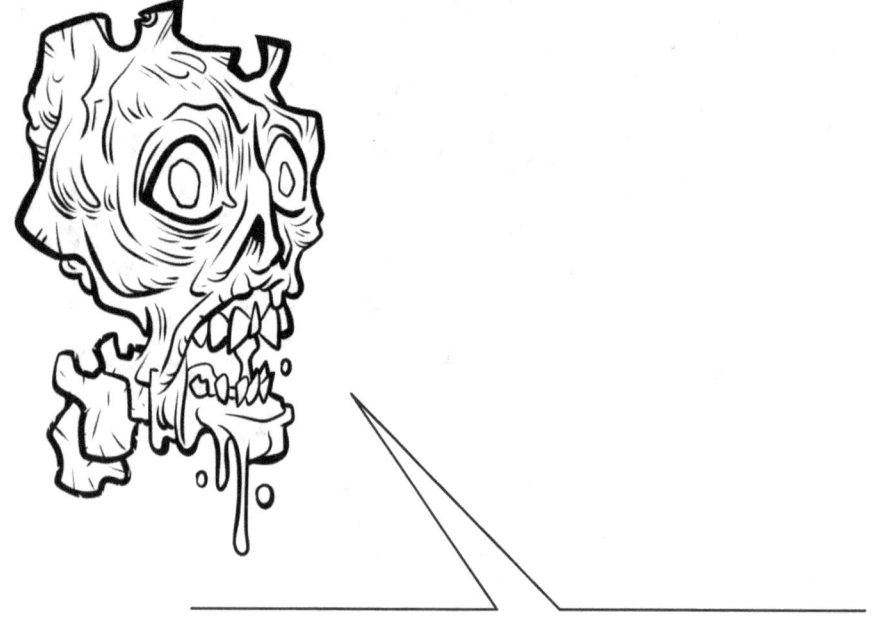

A FEAST FOR THREE.

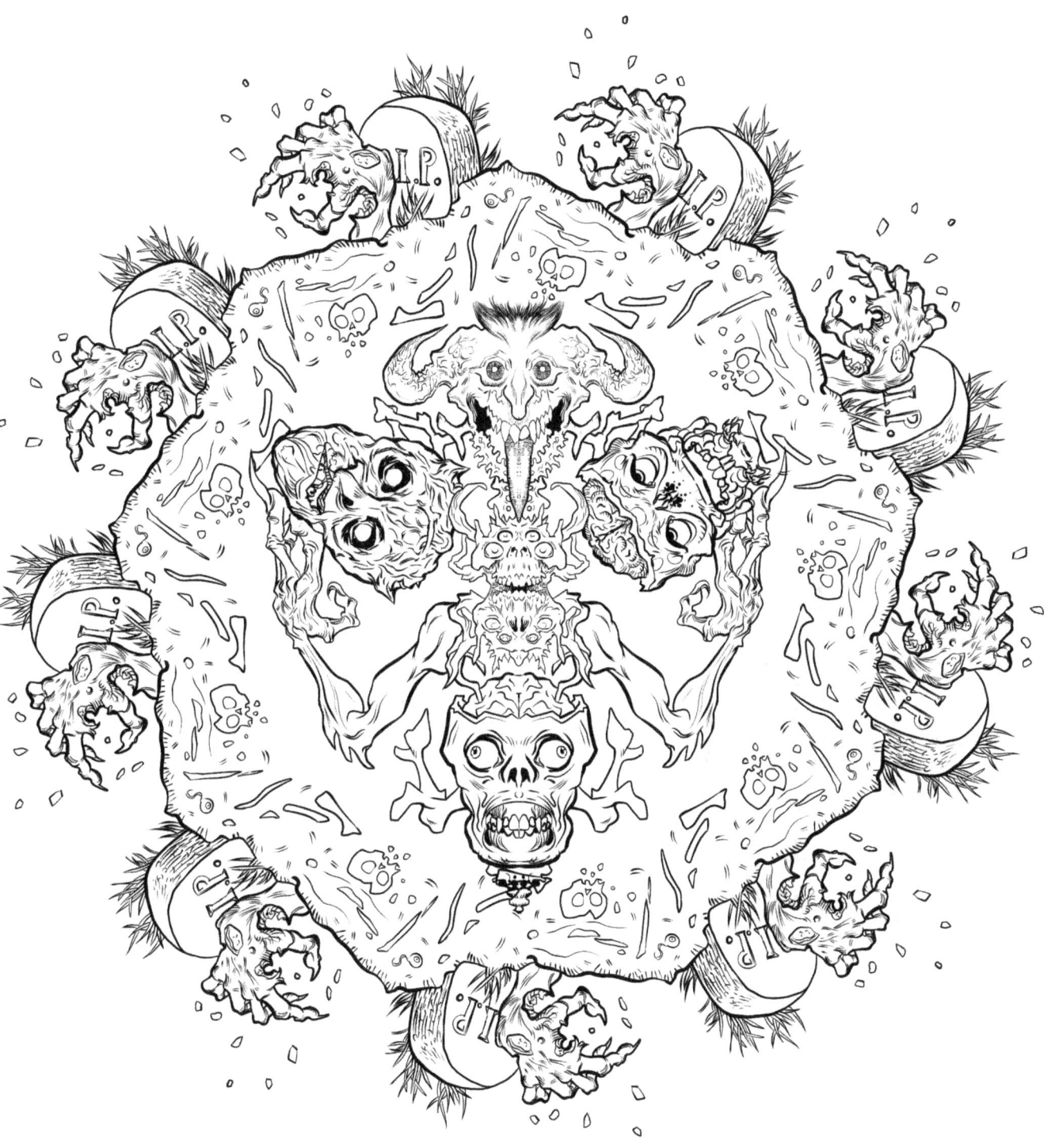

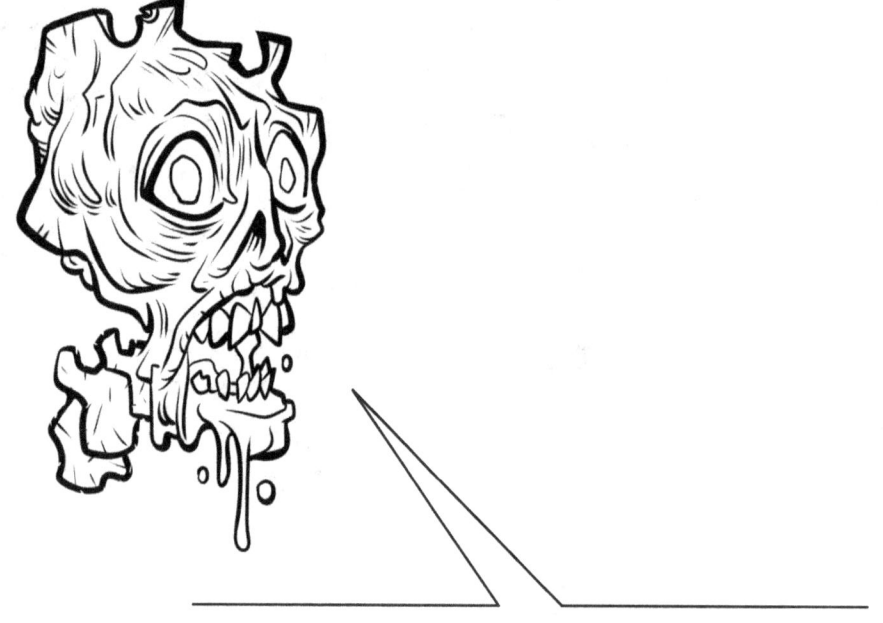

A THIRD EYEFUL.

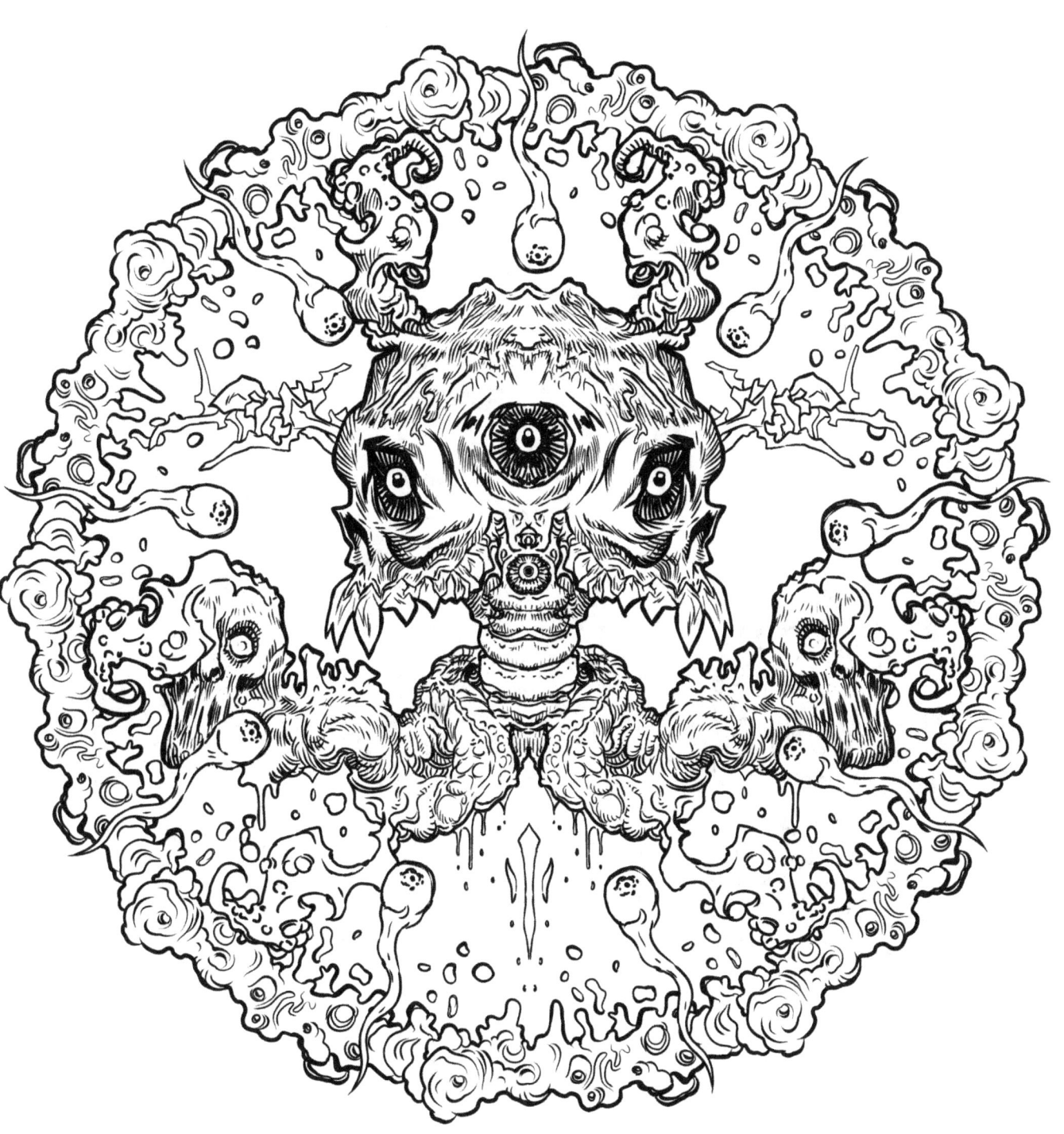

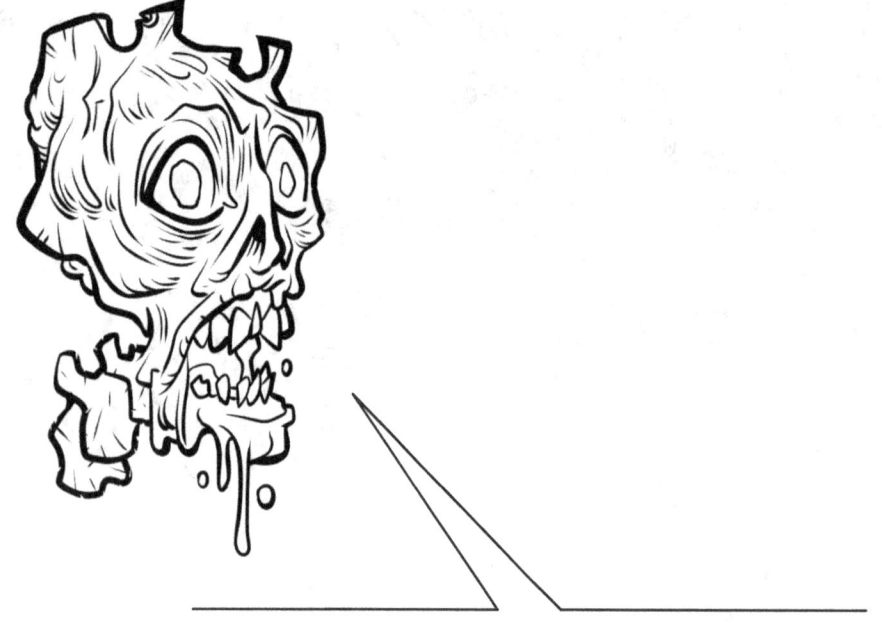

A GOREFUL SYMPHONY.

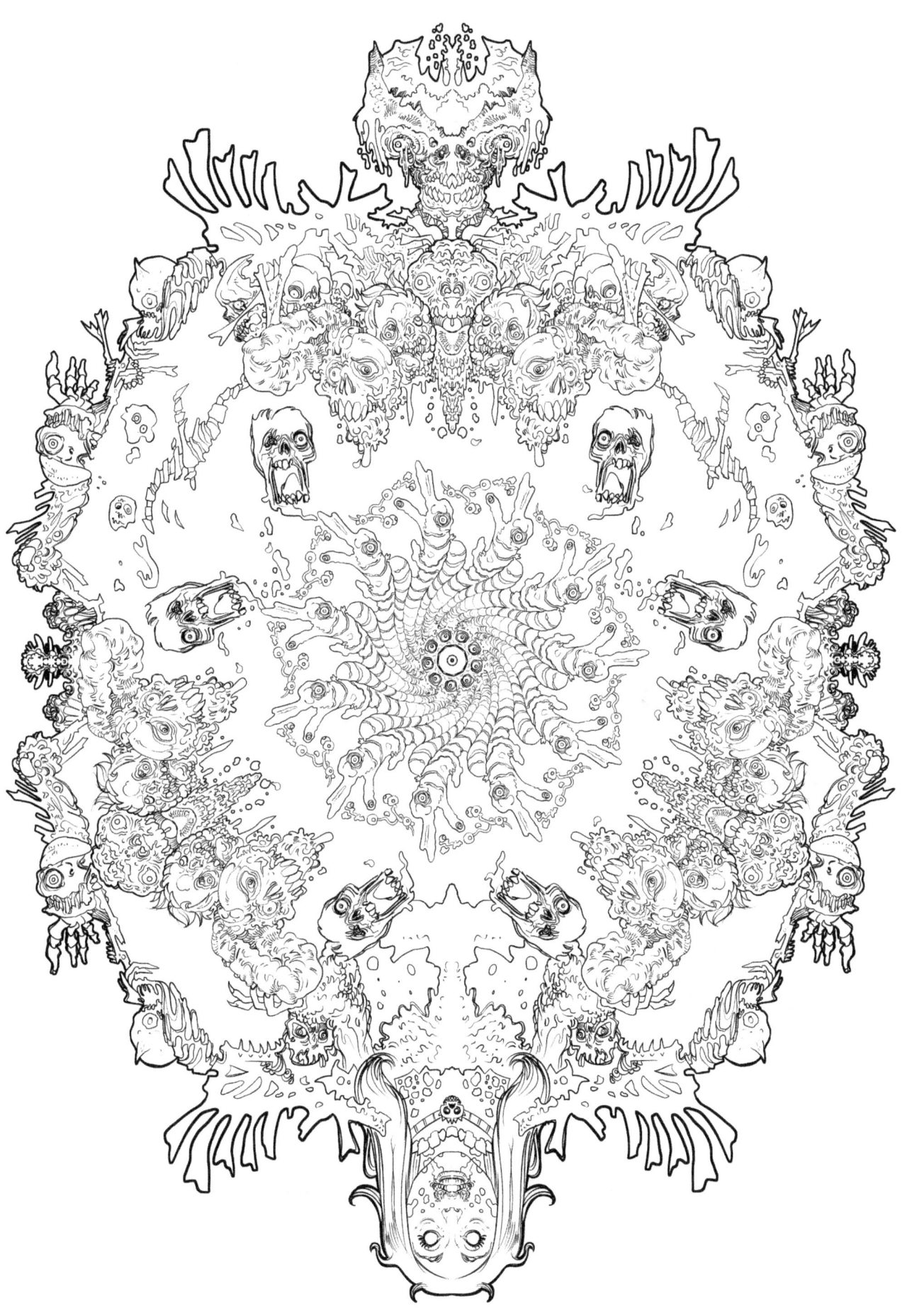

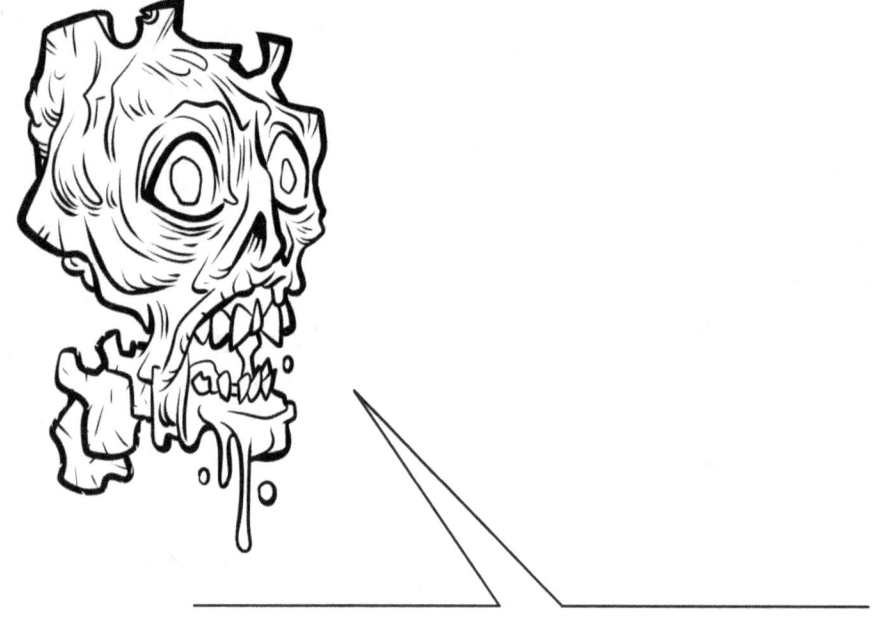

A ROBUST CONTUSION.

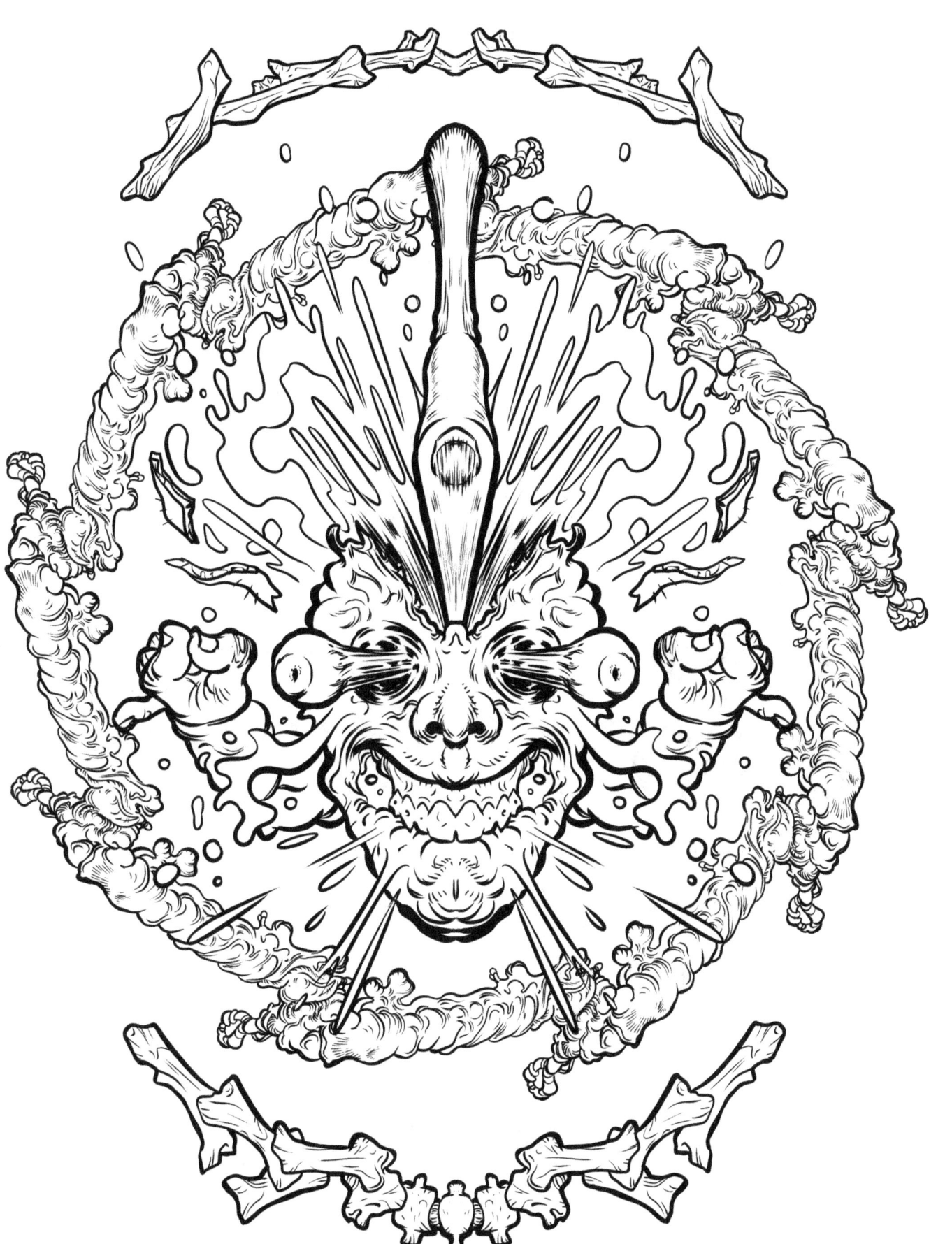

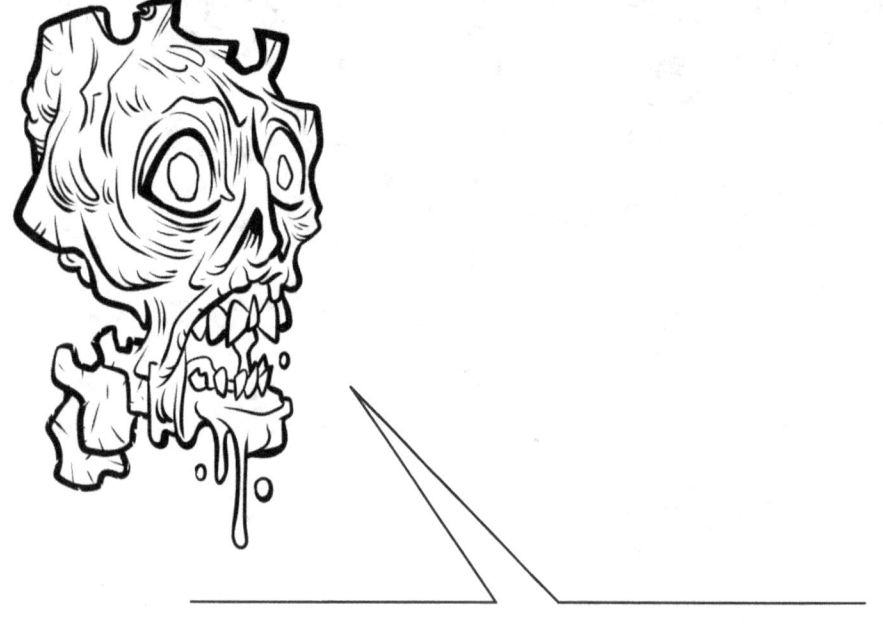

A TIME TO REAP.

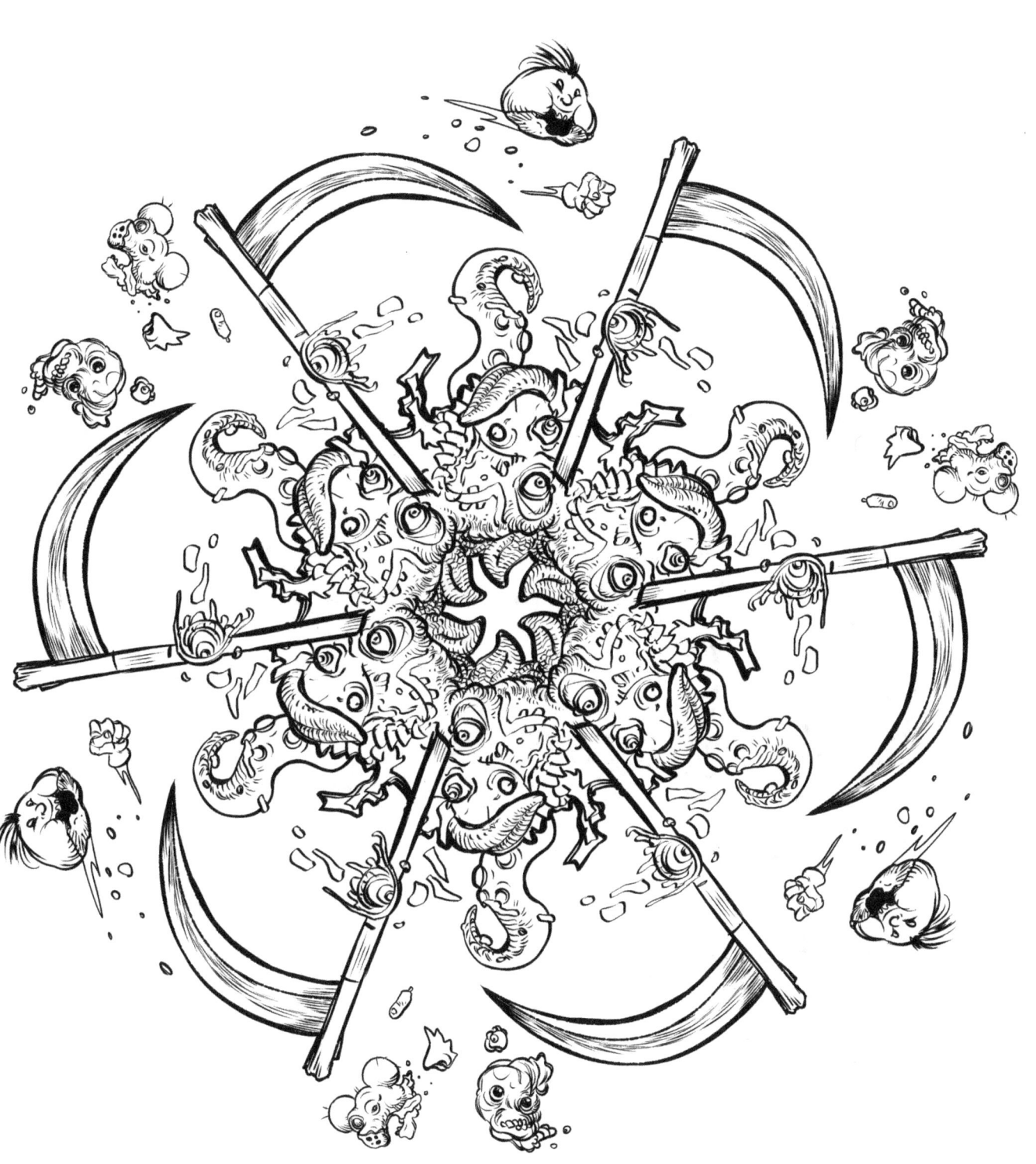

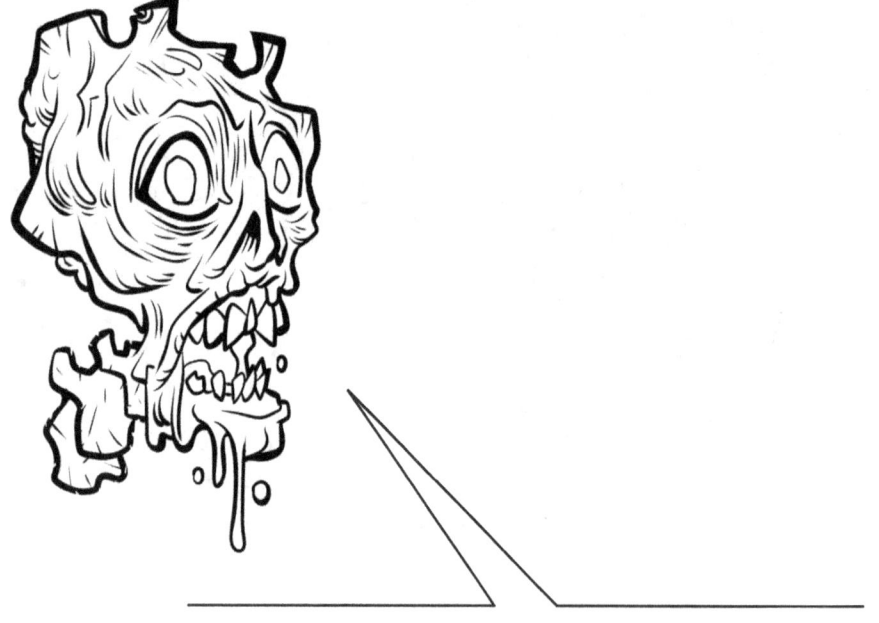

A VICIOUS VISITOR.

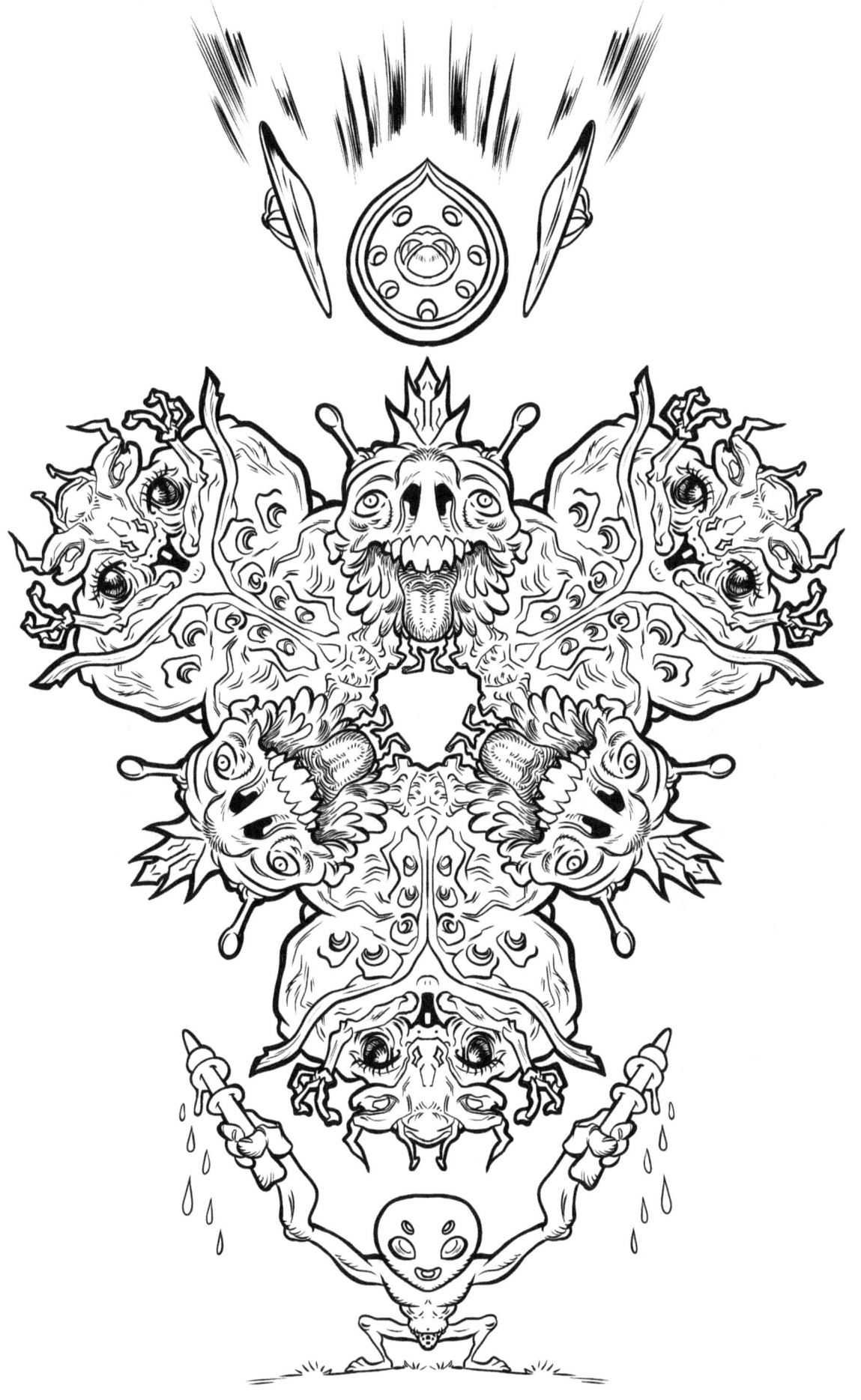

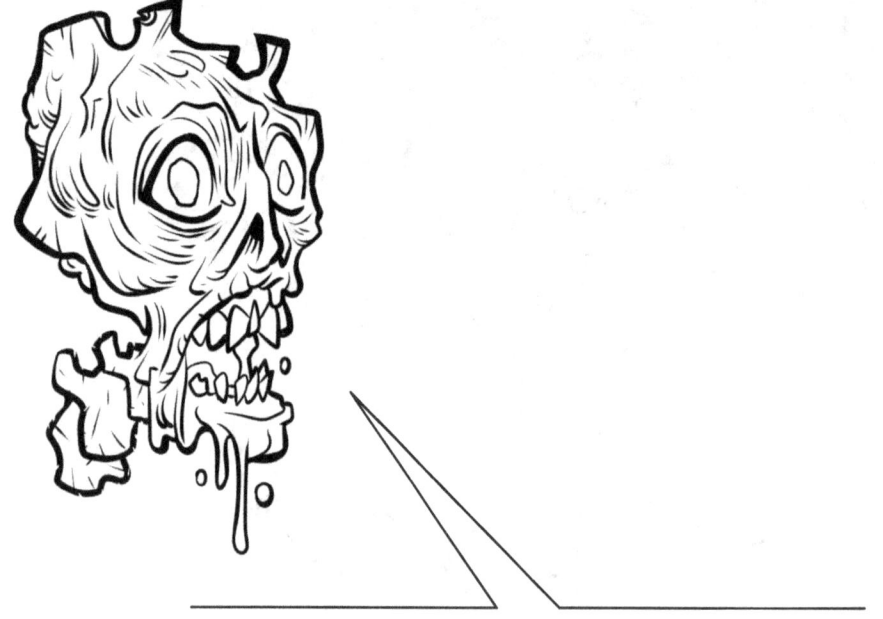

A OSTENTATIOUS TENTACLE.

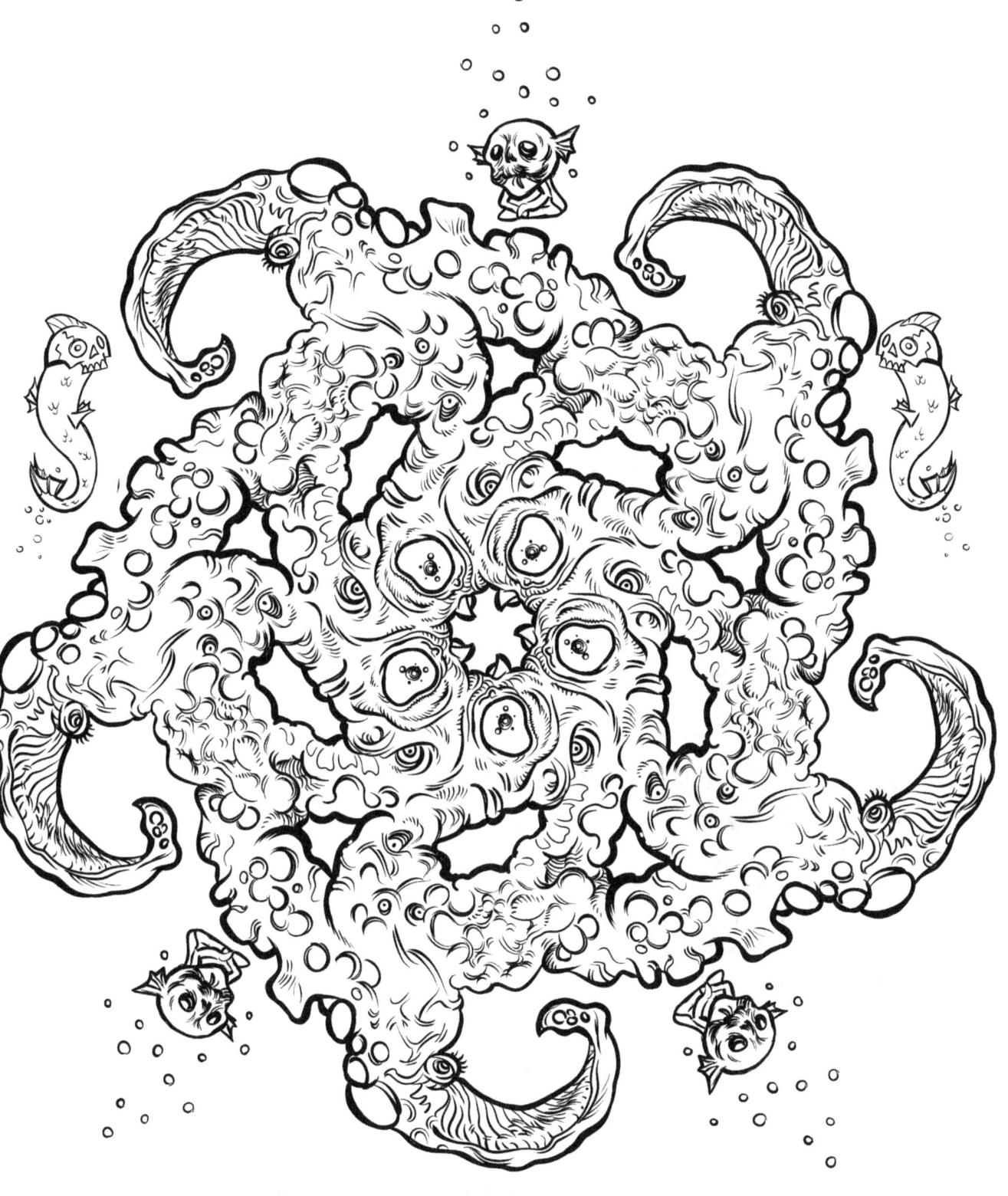

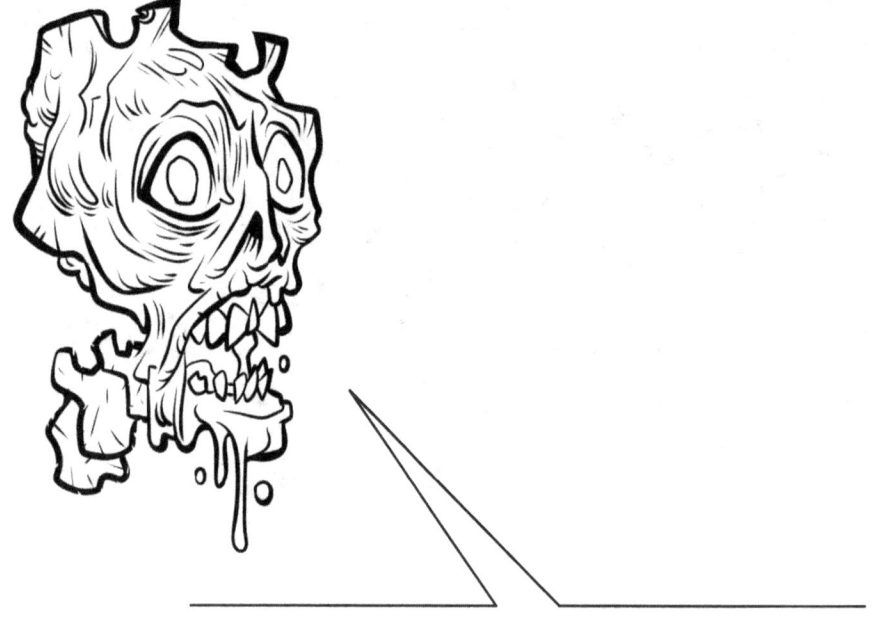

A UNEXPECTED SOJOURN.

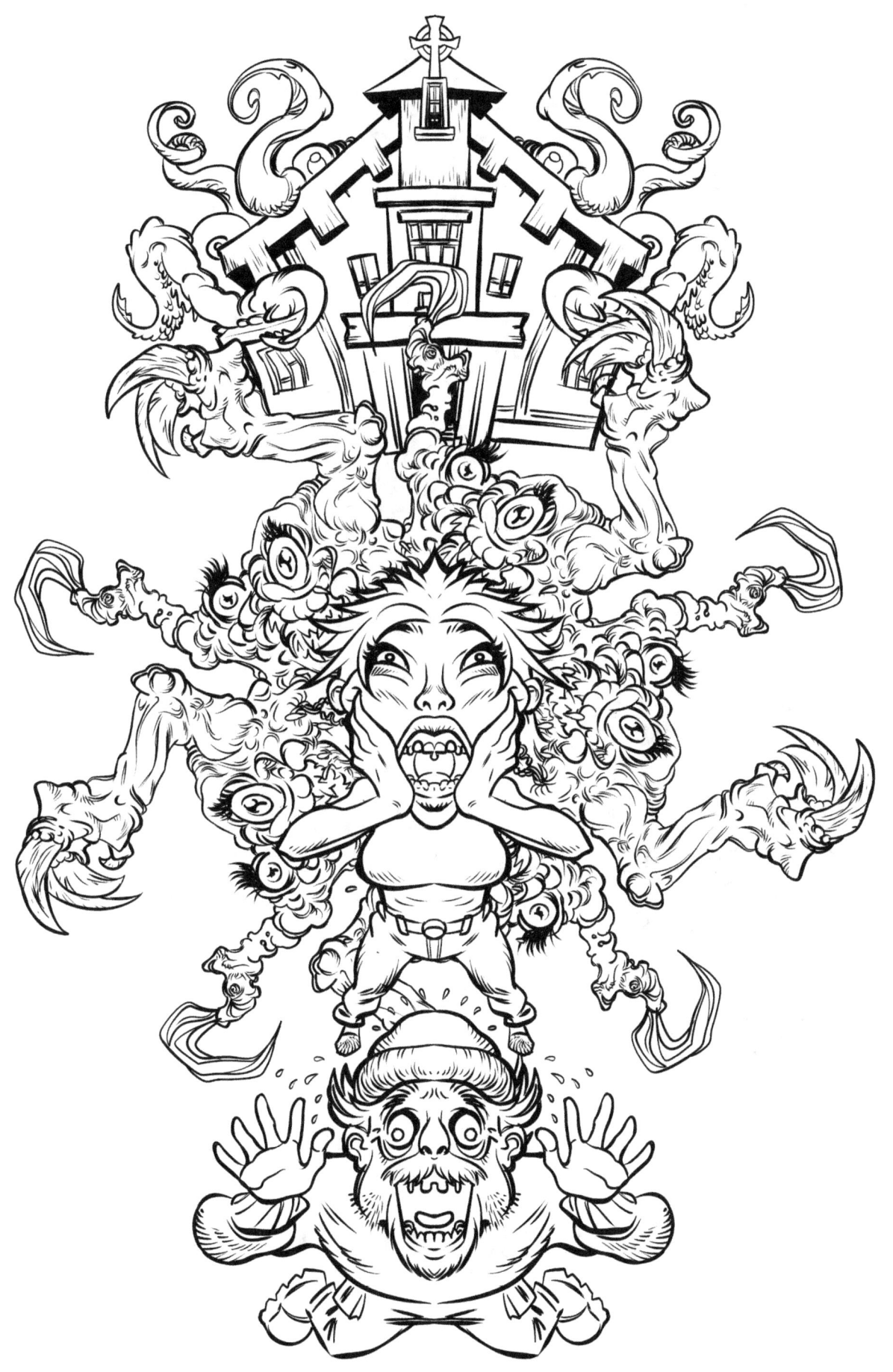

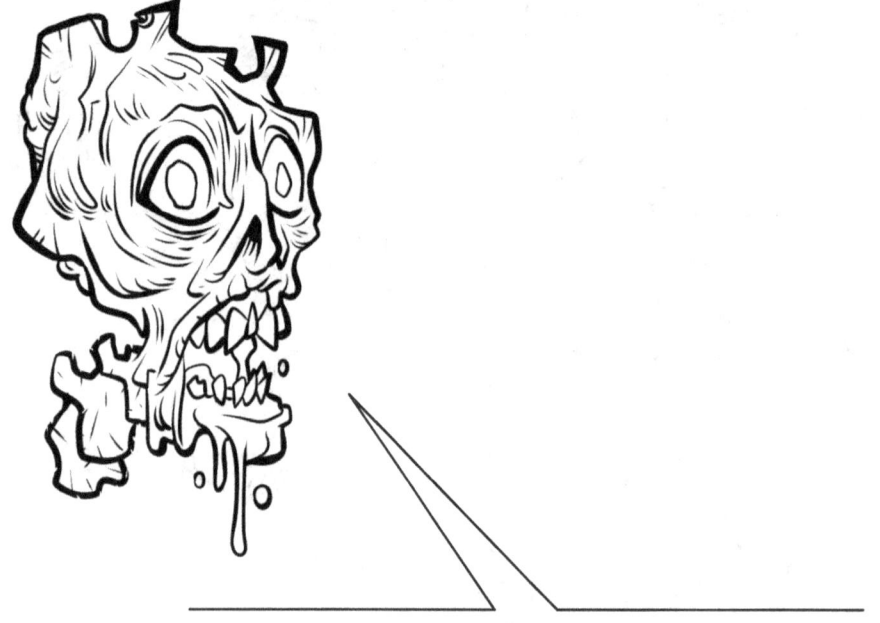

A NEVER ENDING BITE.

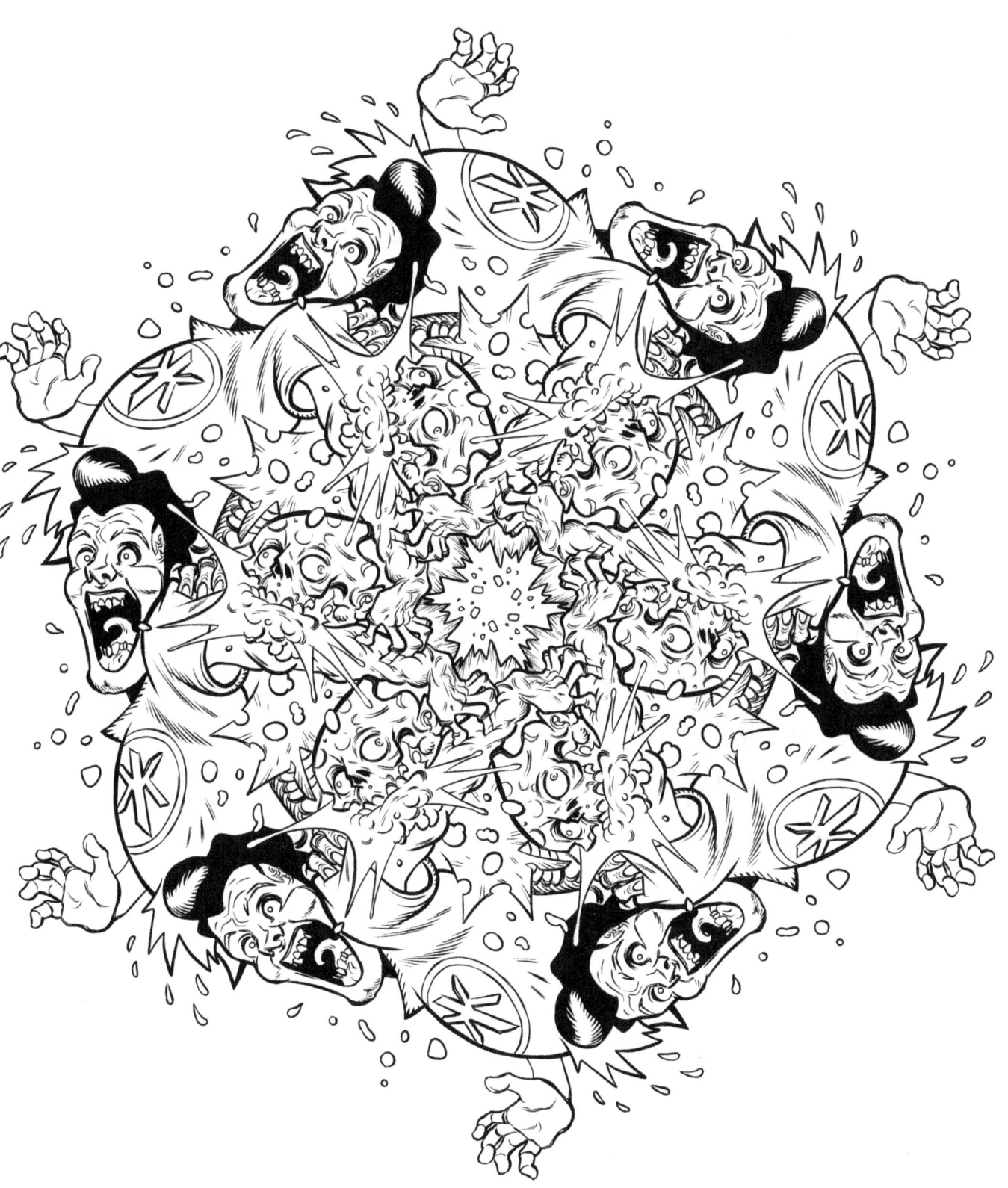

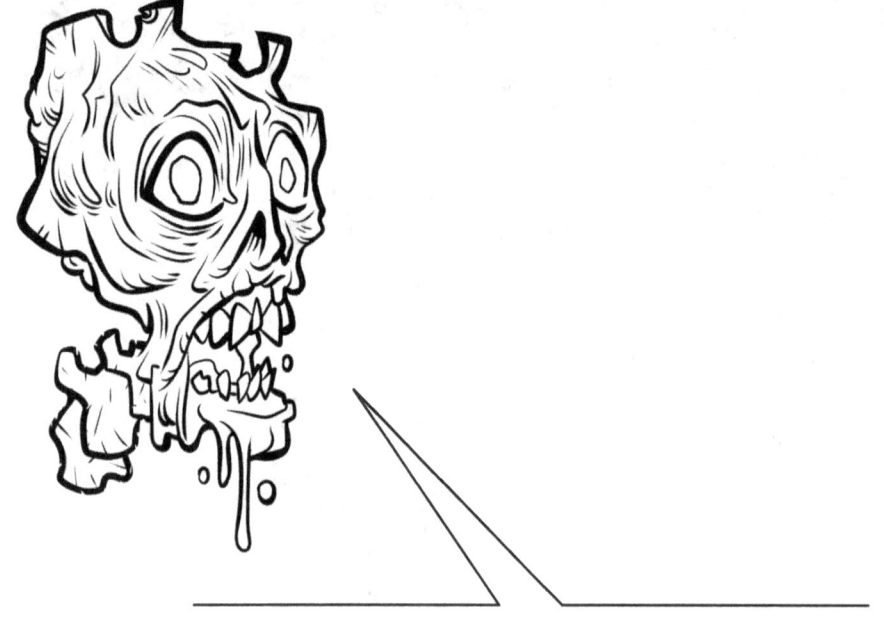

A BOOK SPEAKS.

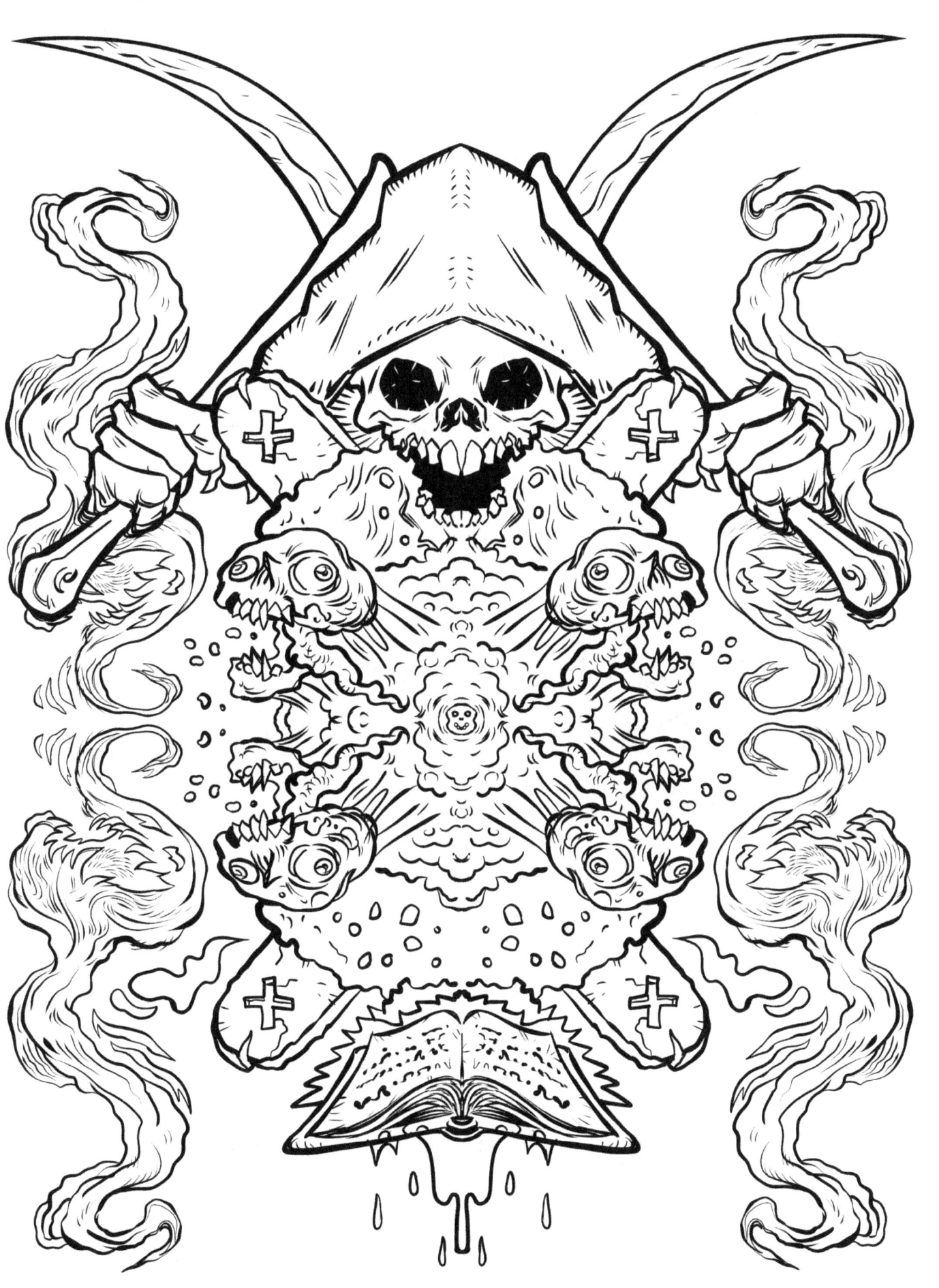

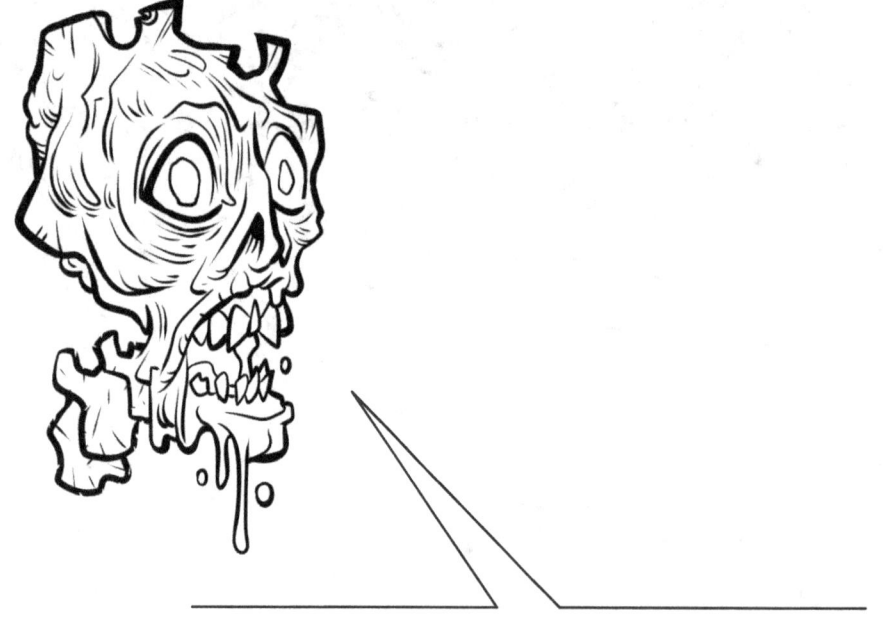

A HEART IN THE RIGHT HANDS.

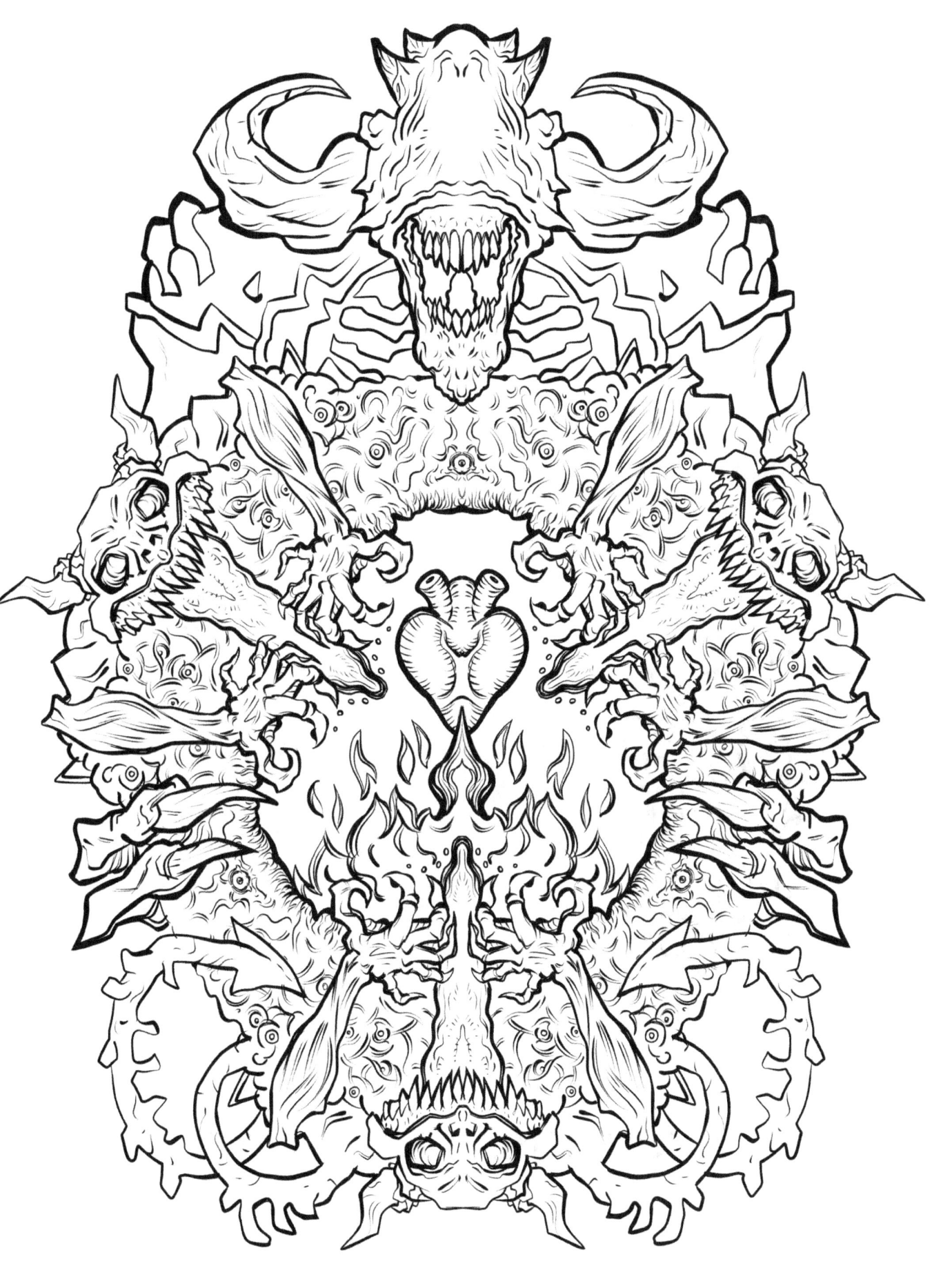

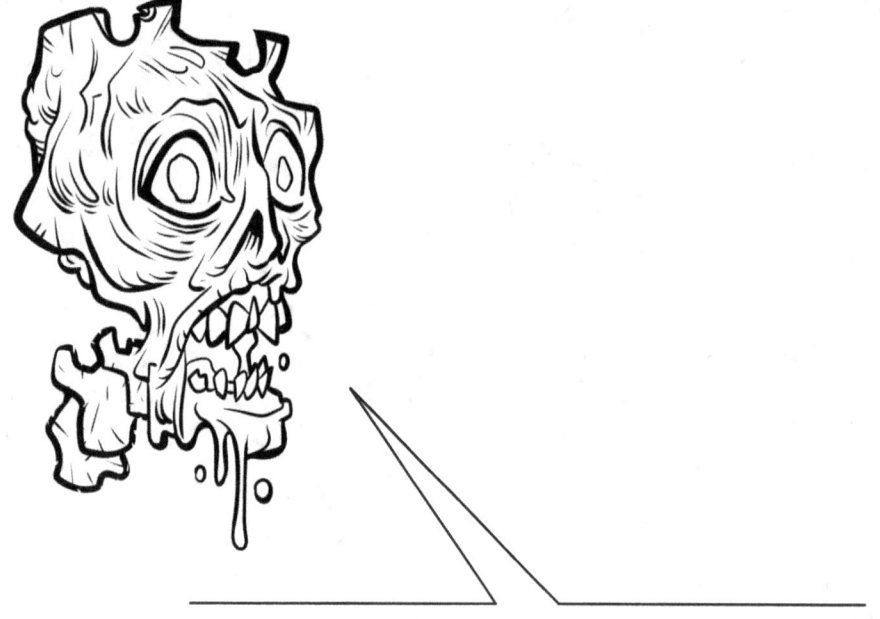

A COLORFUL CONCENTRATE.

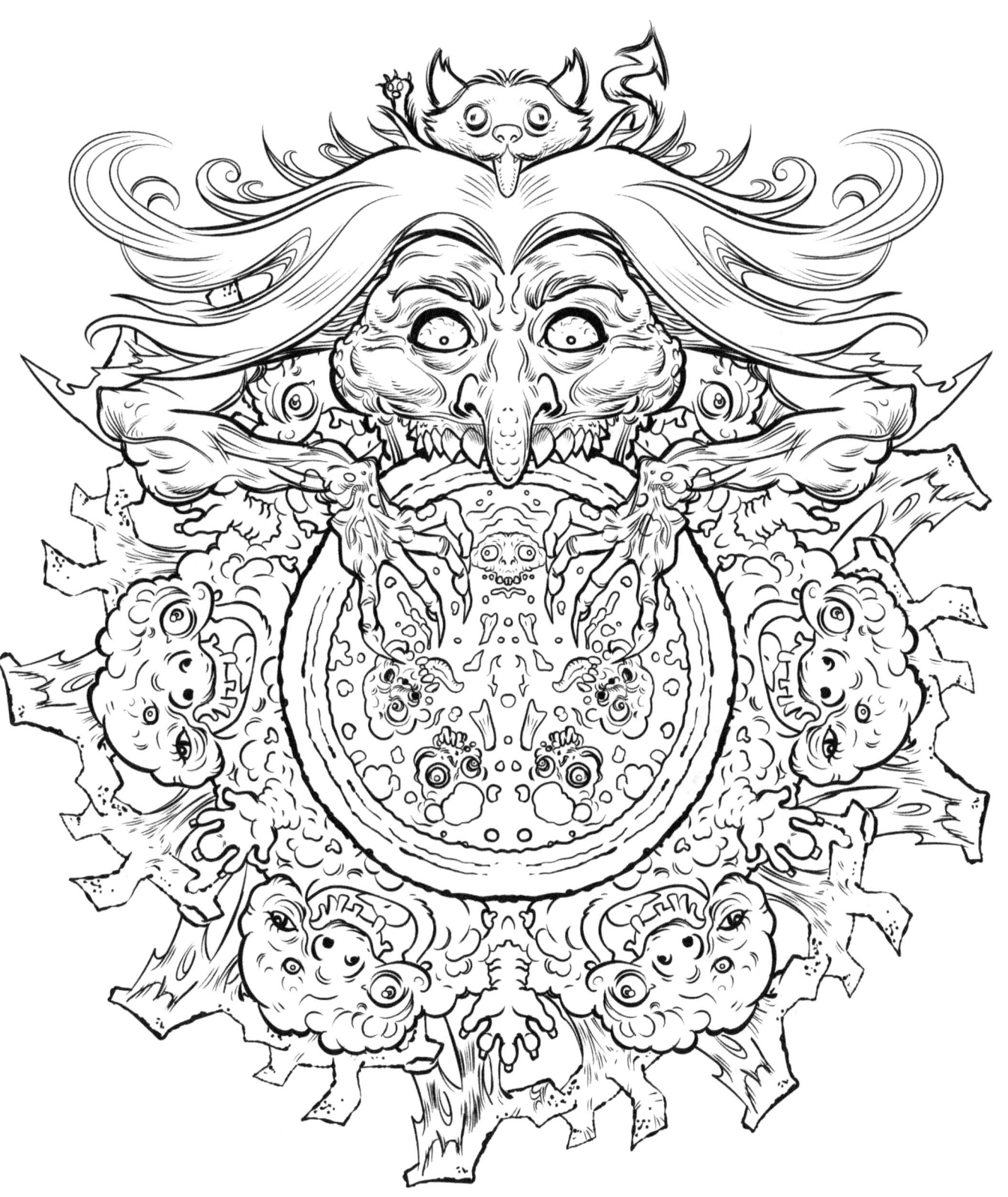

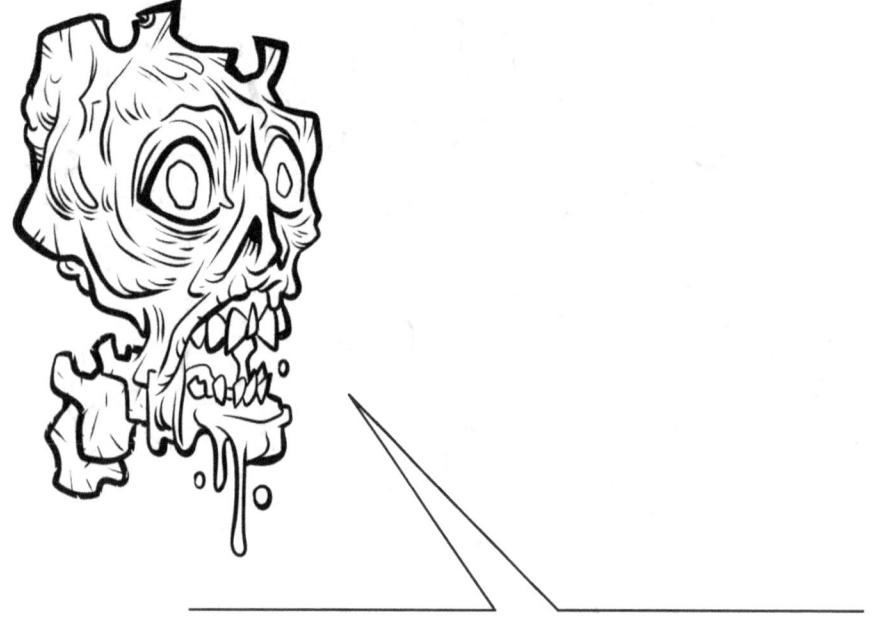

A RADIOACTIVE ACTIVITY.

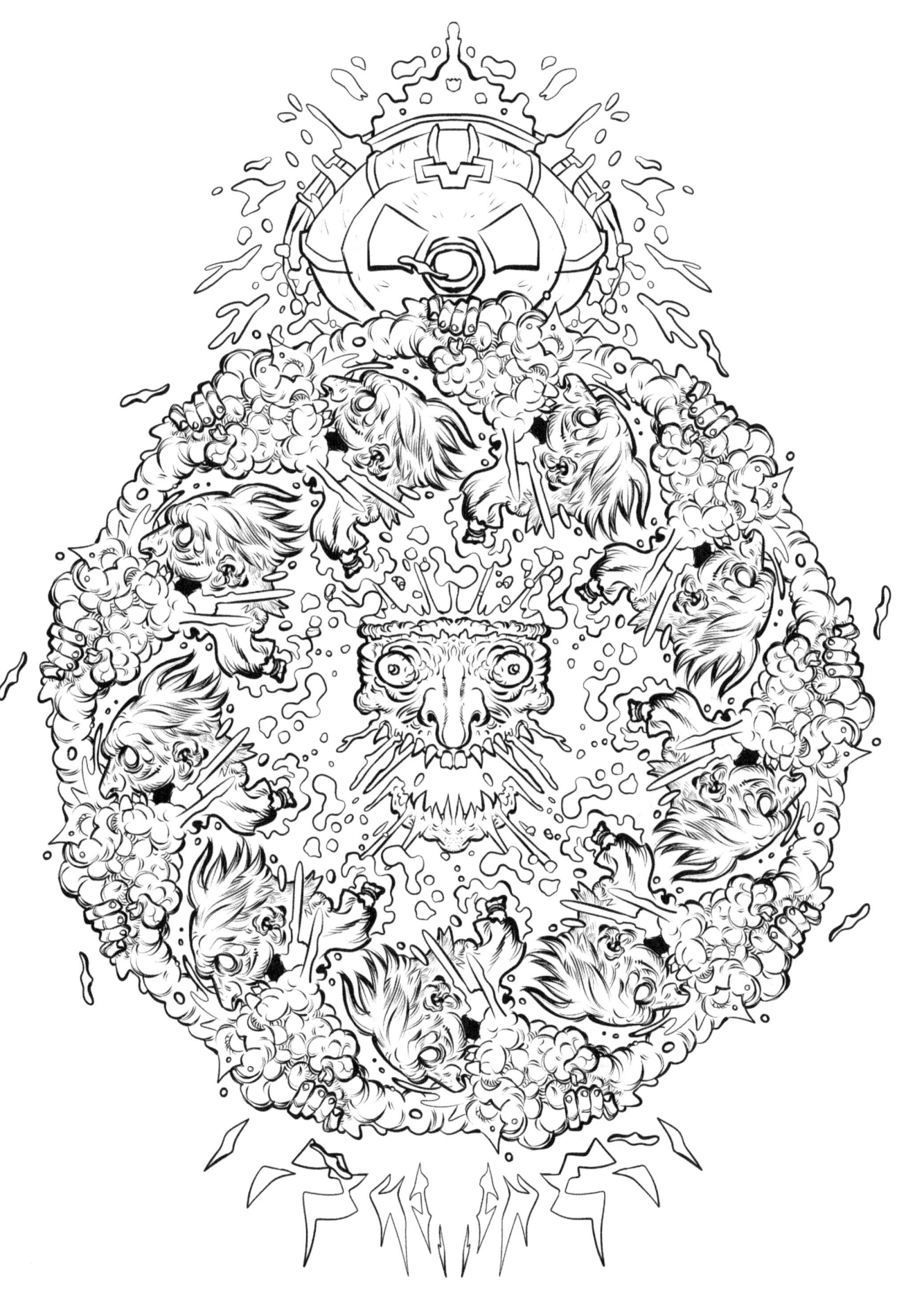

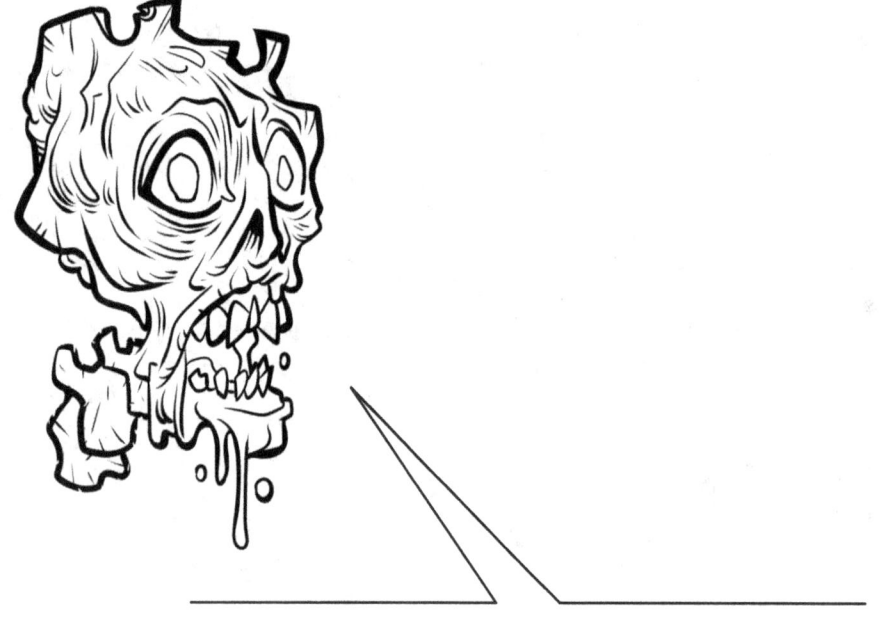

A GUTSY CHARADE.

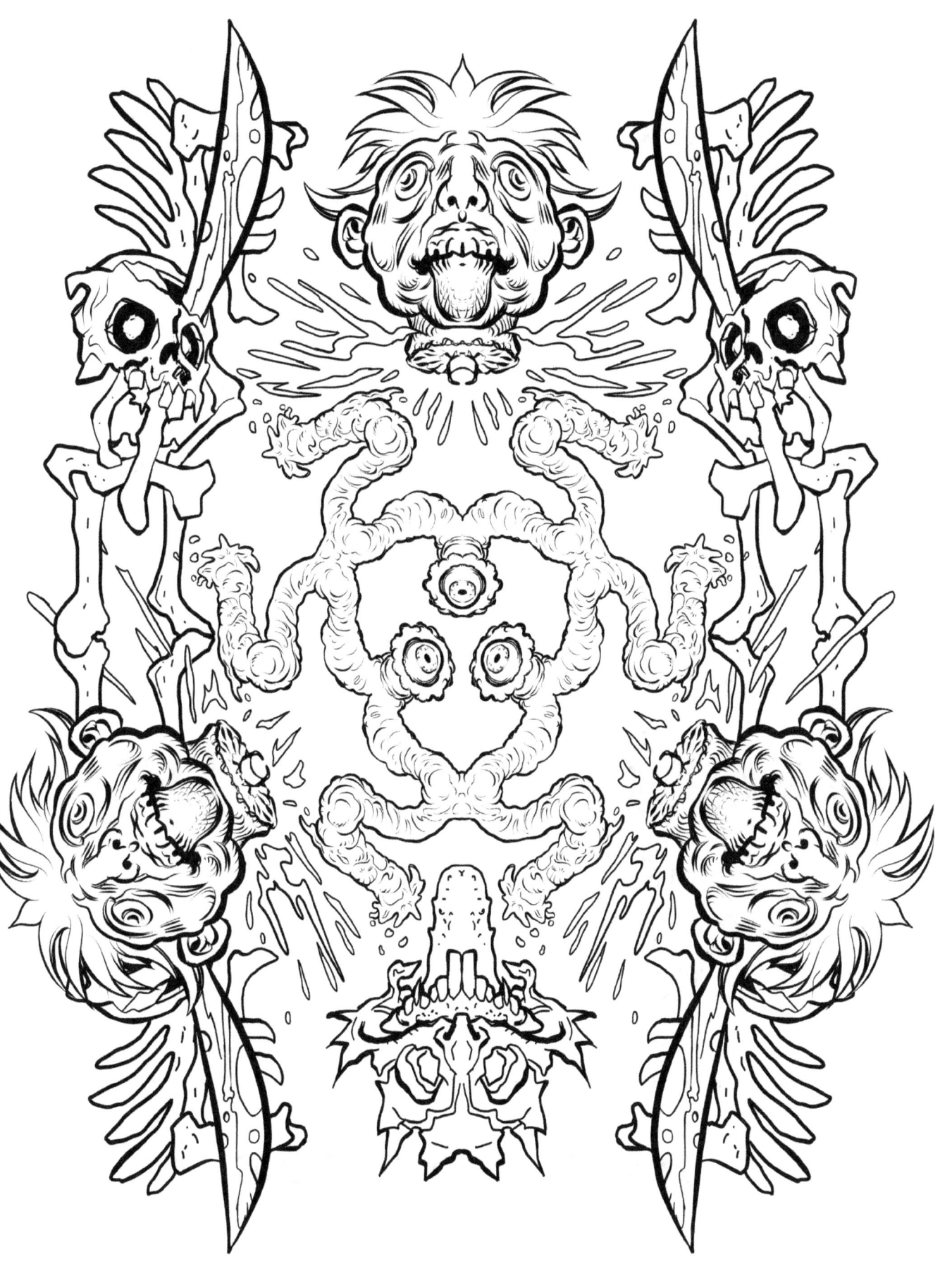

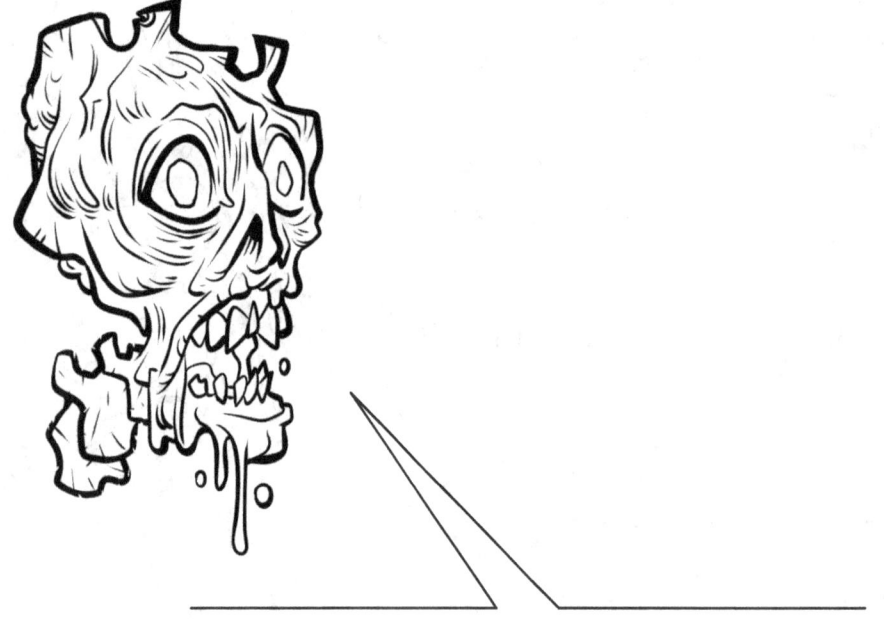

A TURBULENT INCANTATION.

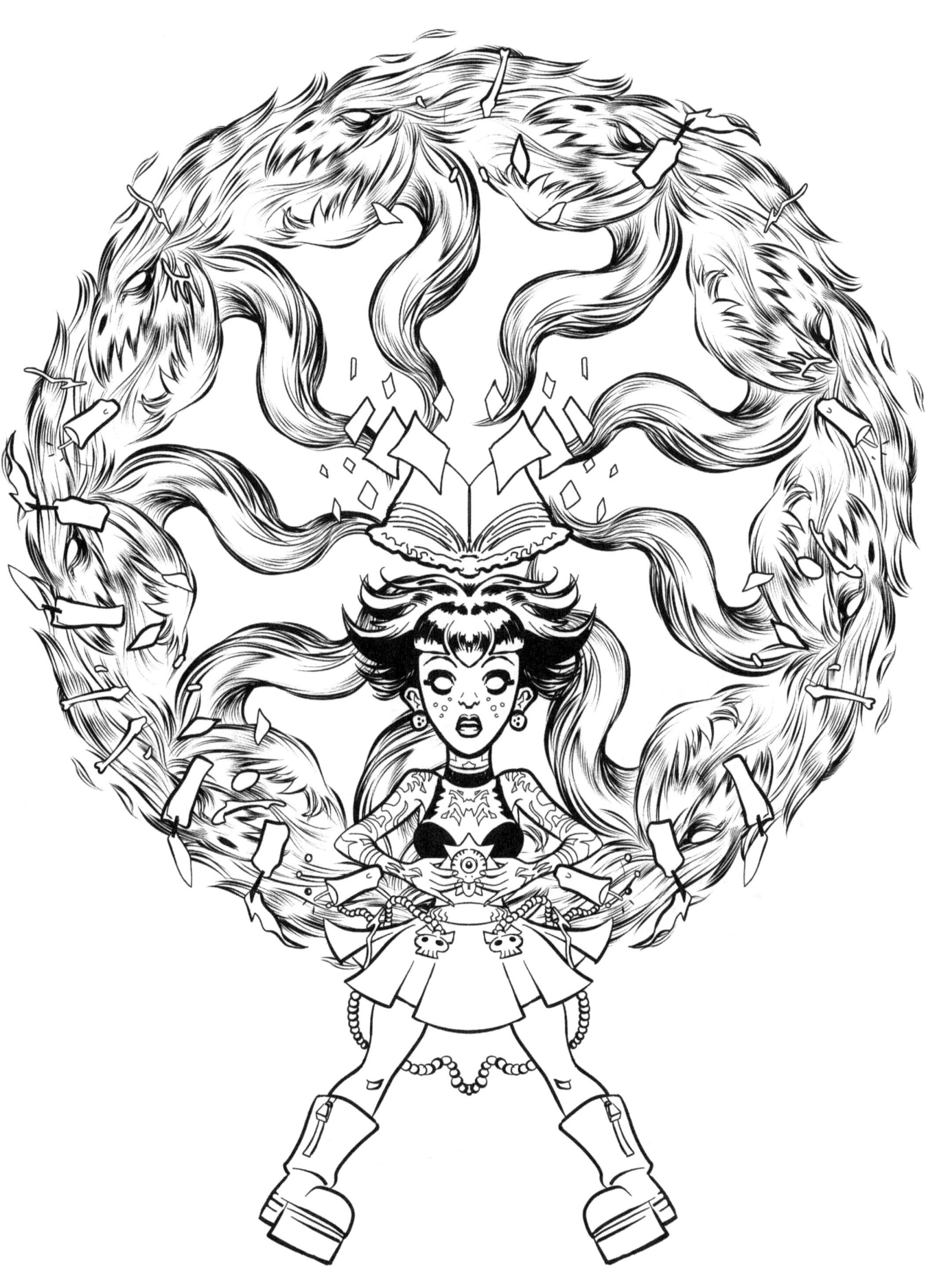

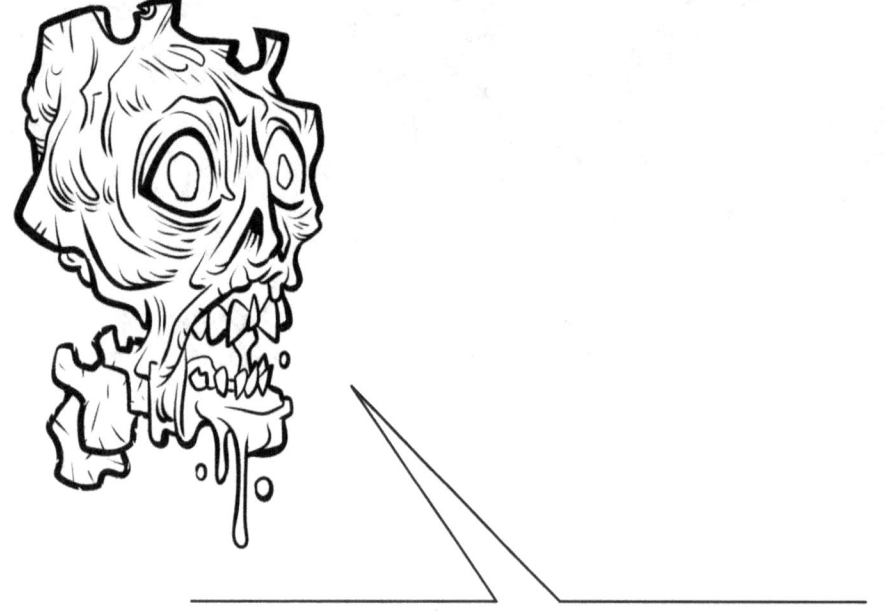

A RECALCITRANT PARASITE.

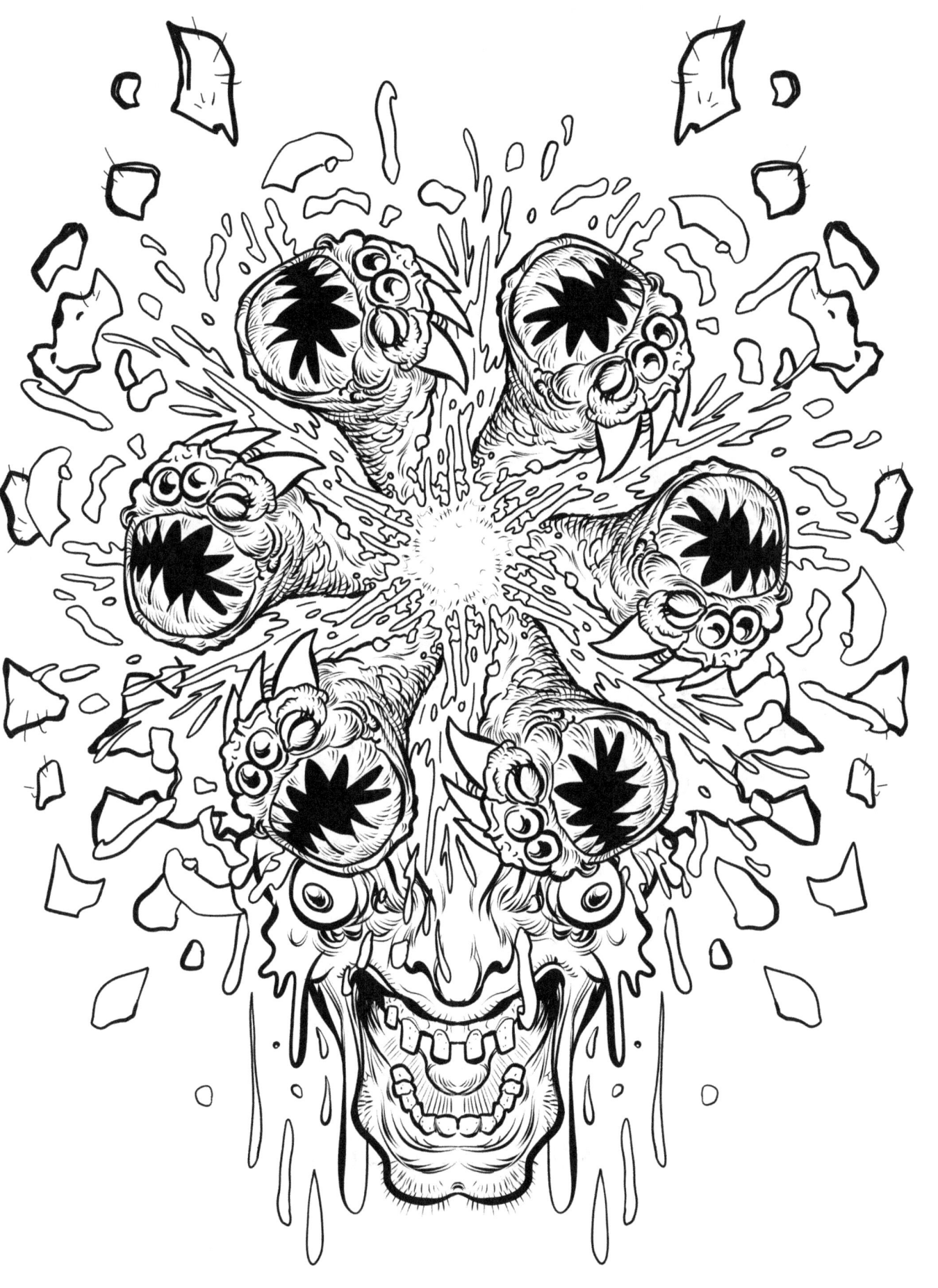

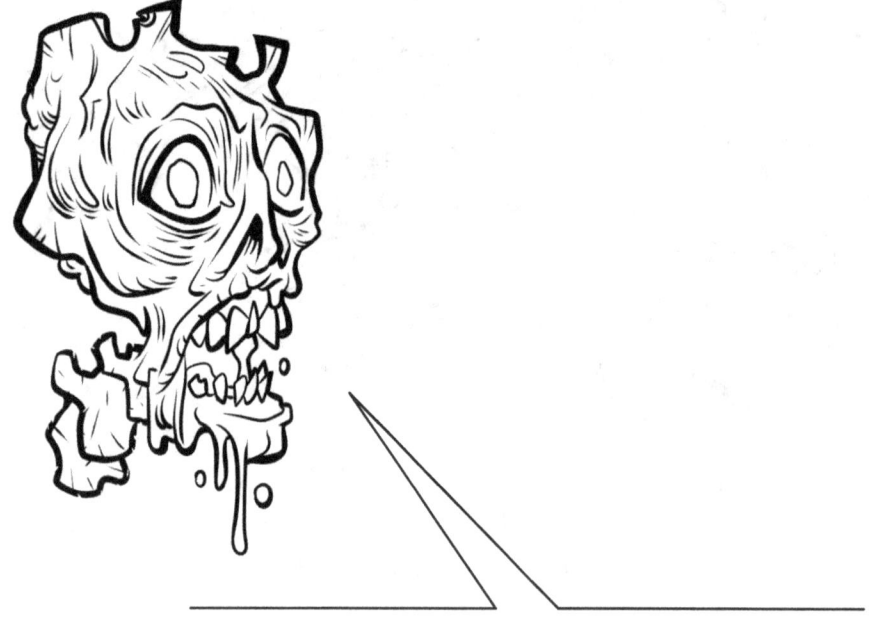

A PRINCESS PRICE.

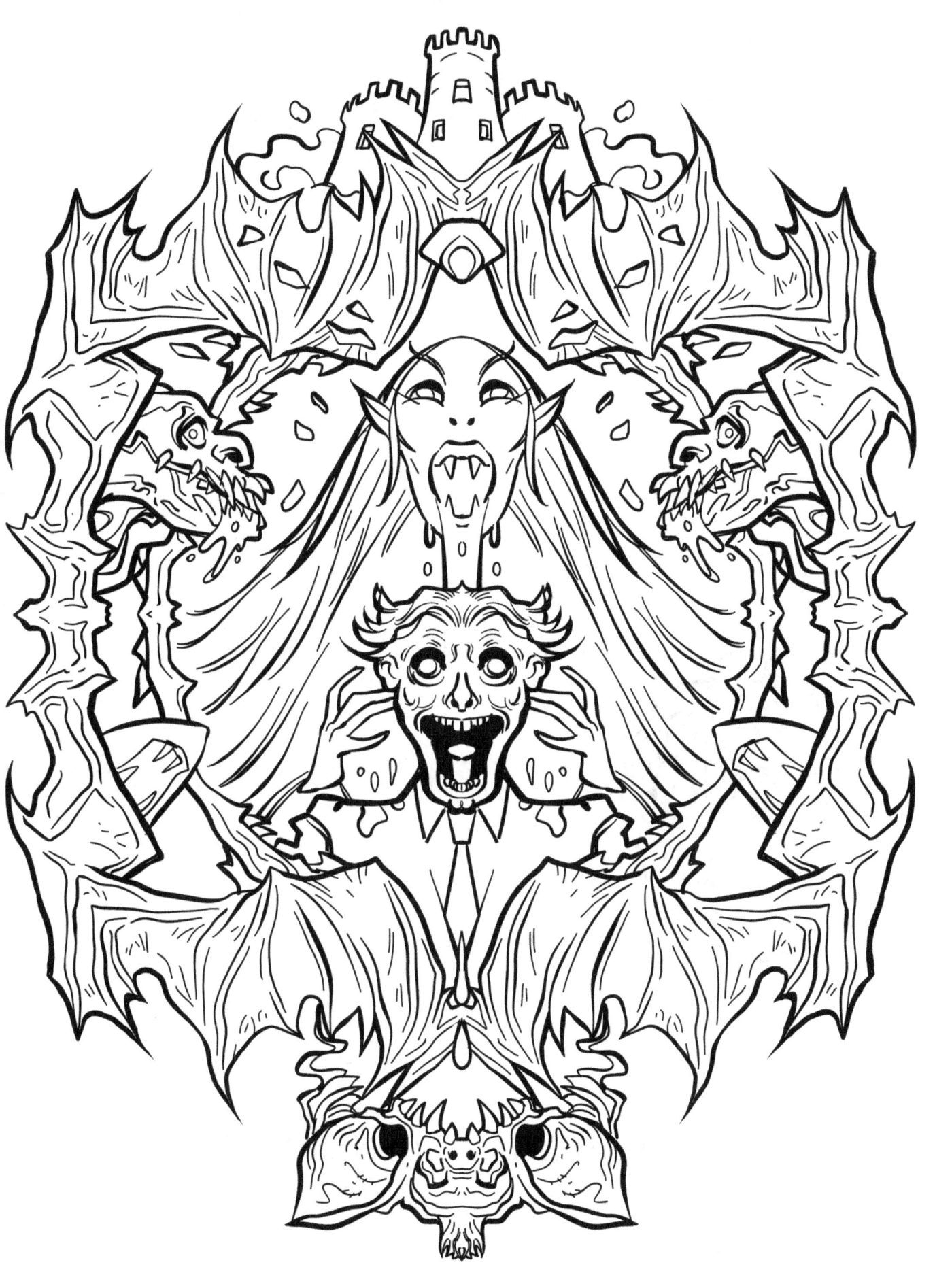

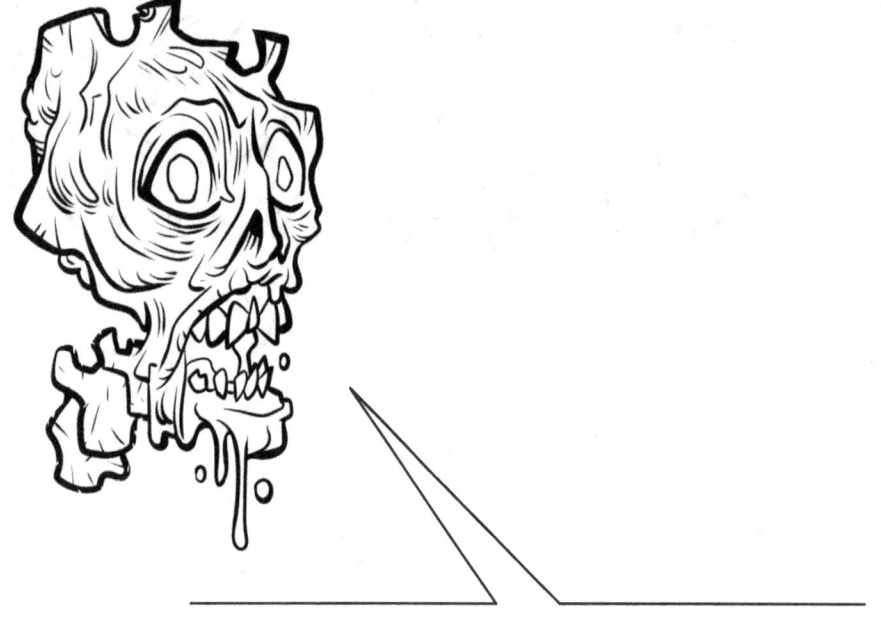

A MEDICINAL ATONEMENT.

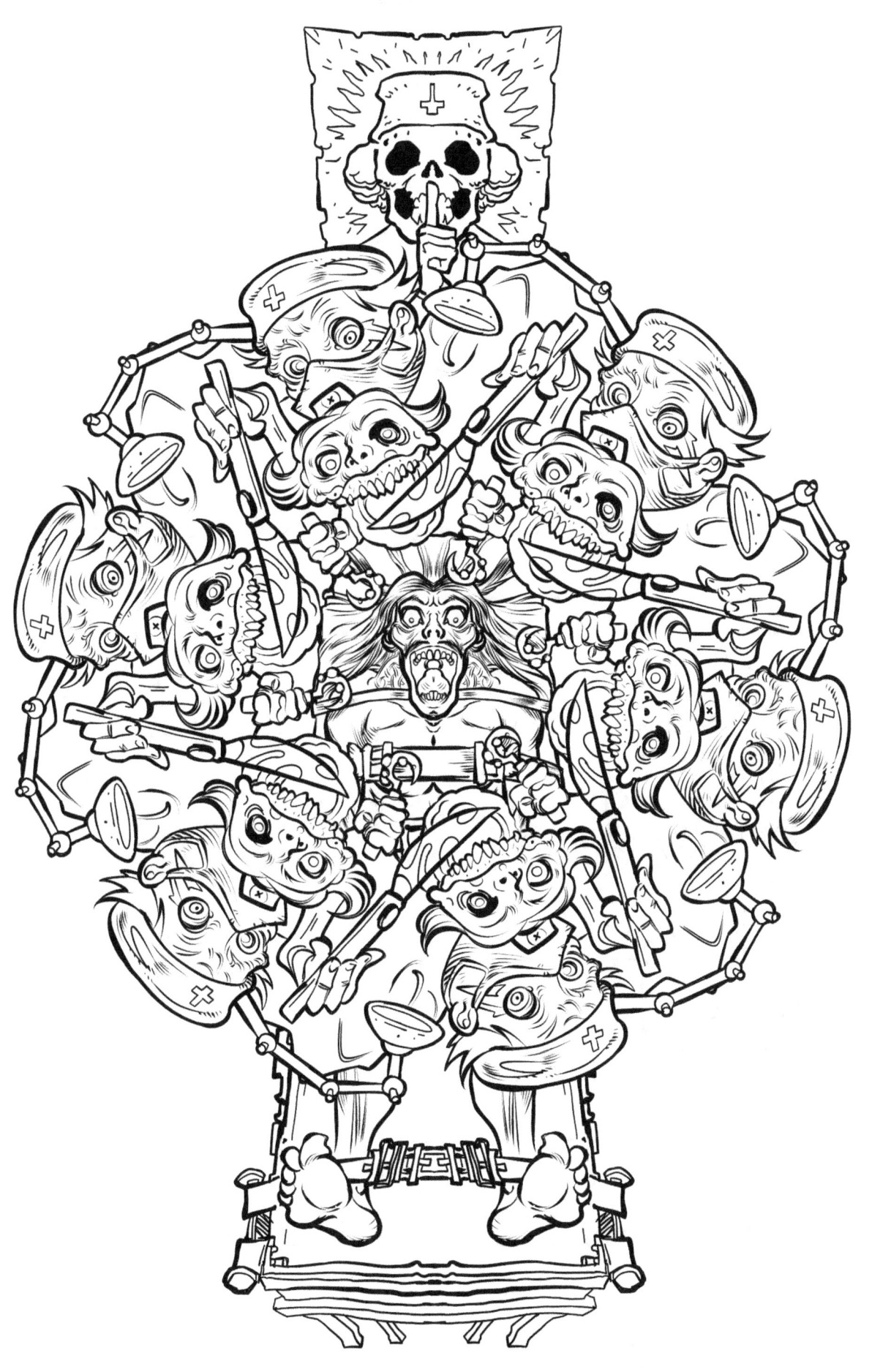

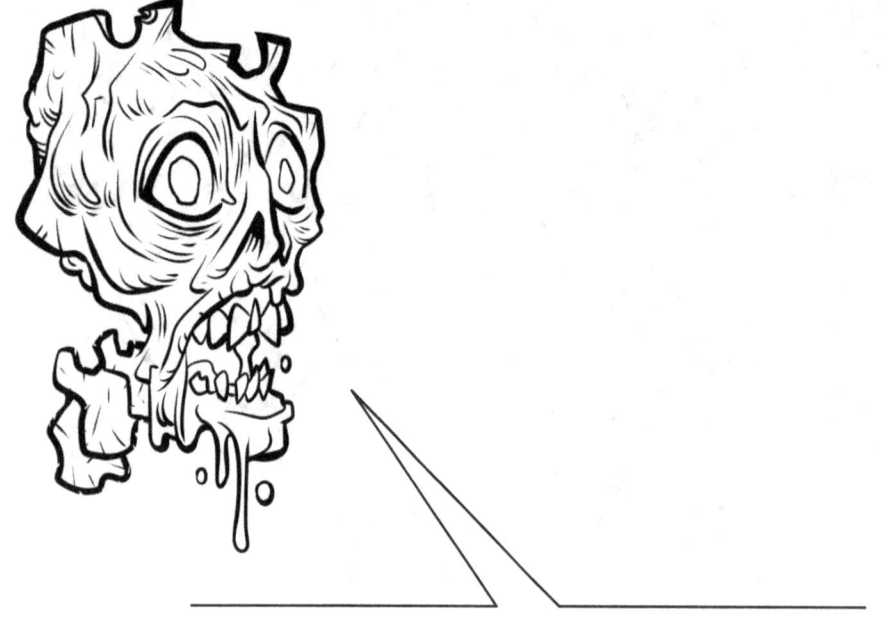

A DISAFFECTED METAMORPHOSIS.

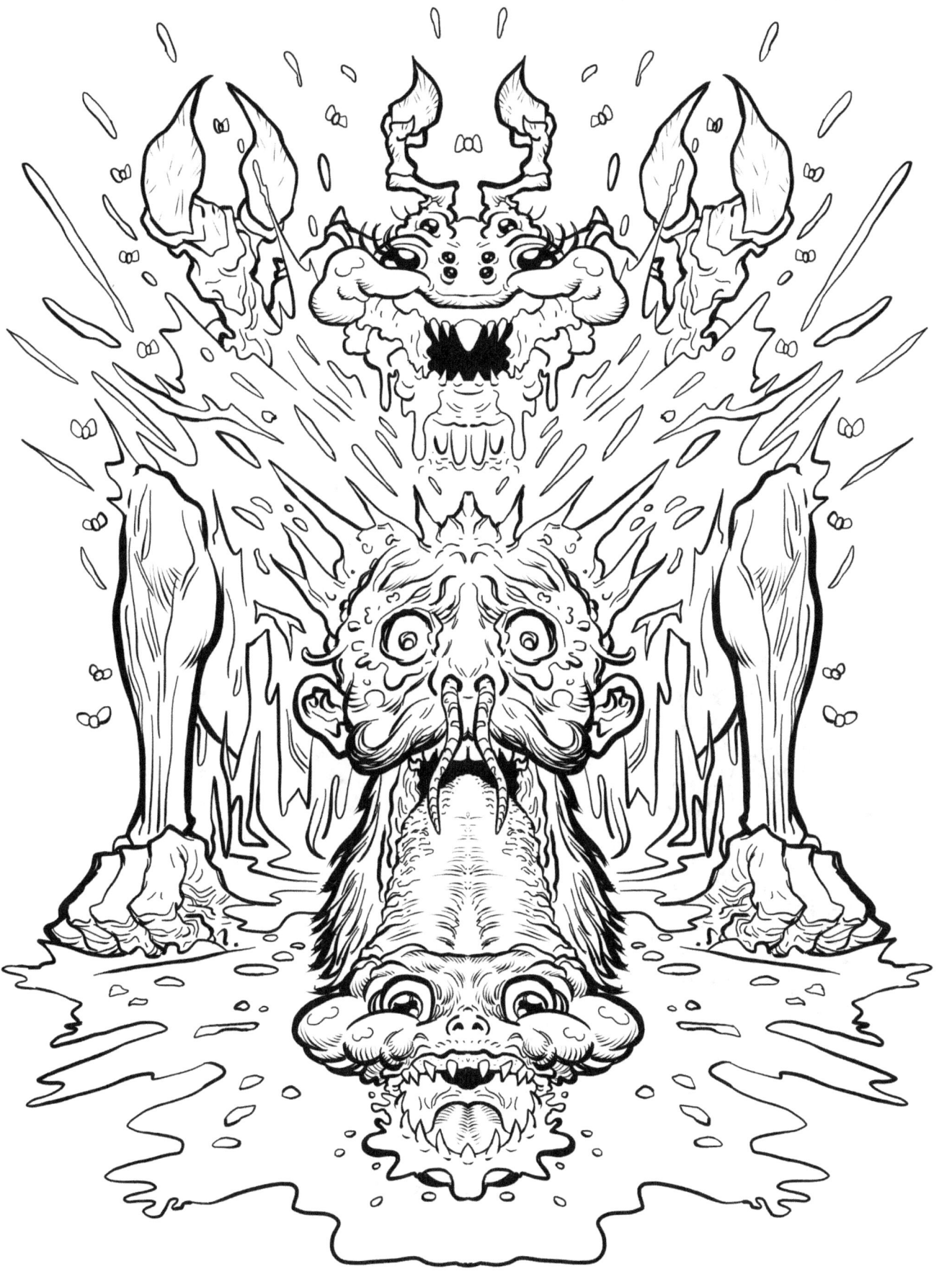

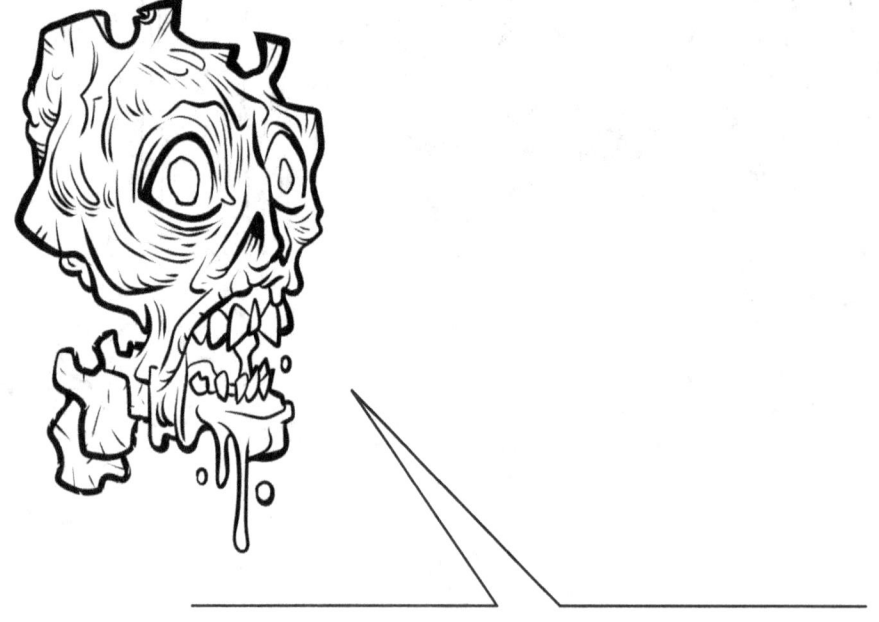

A DIVINATION OF EVIL.

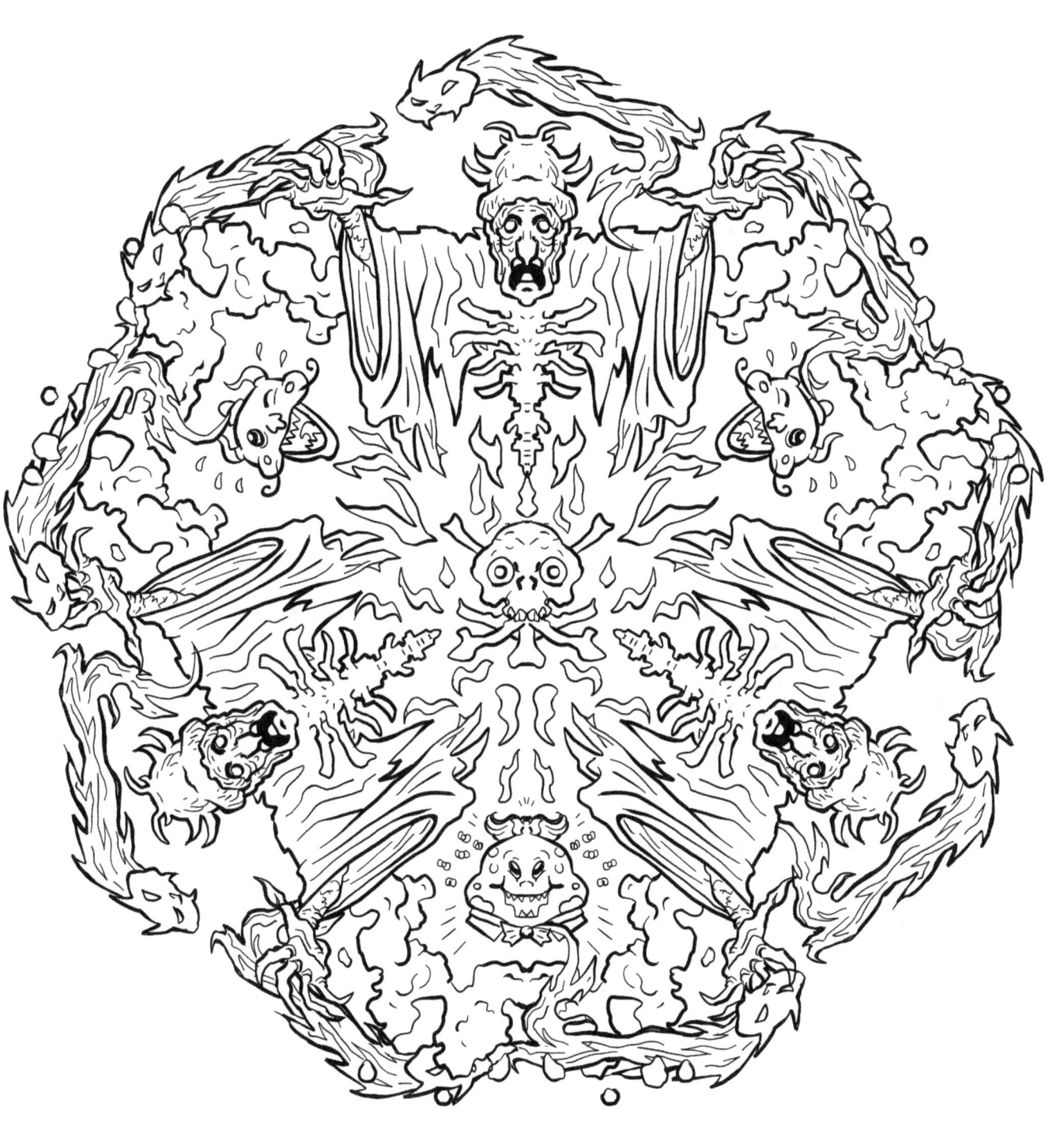

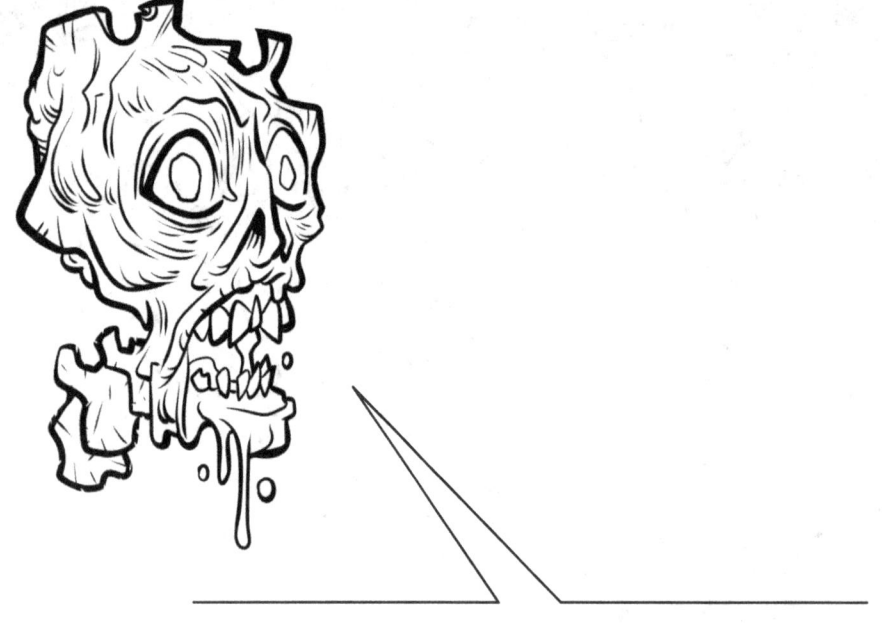

A KID'S GAME.

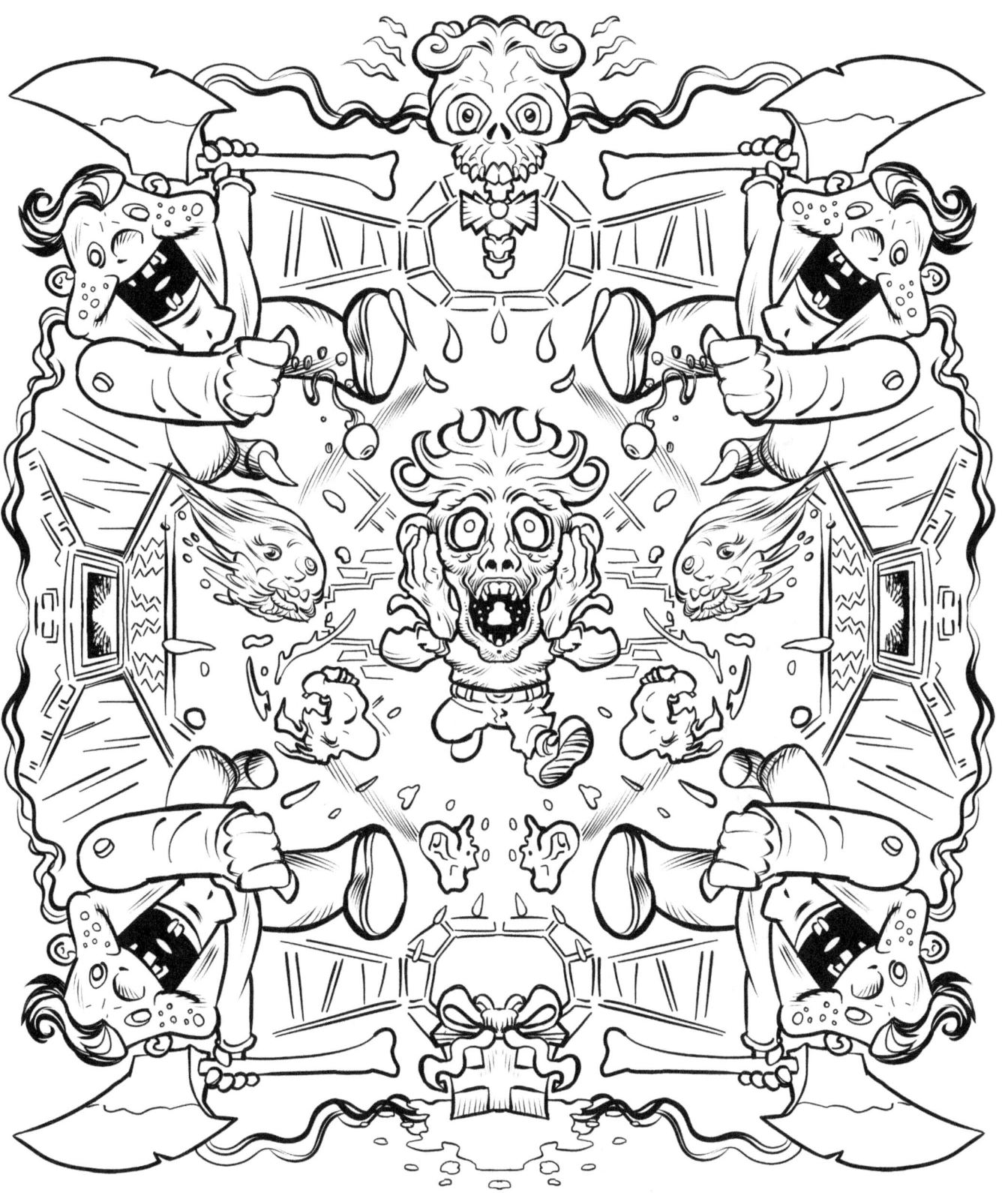

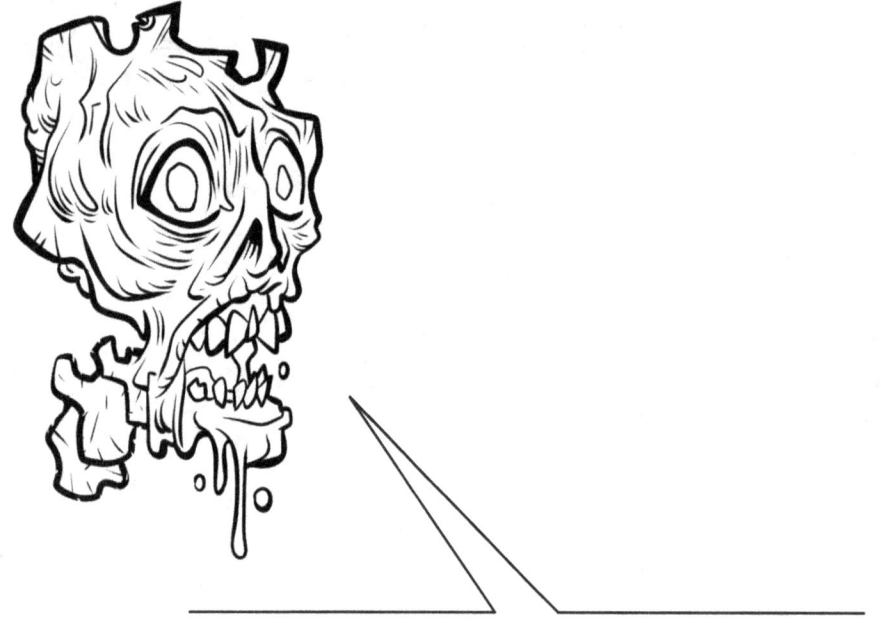

A FEAST IN THE MAKING.

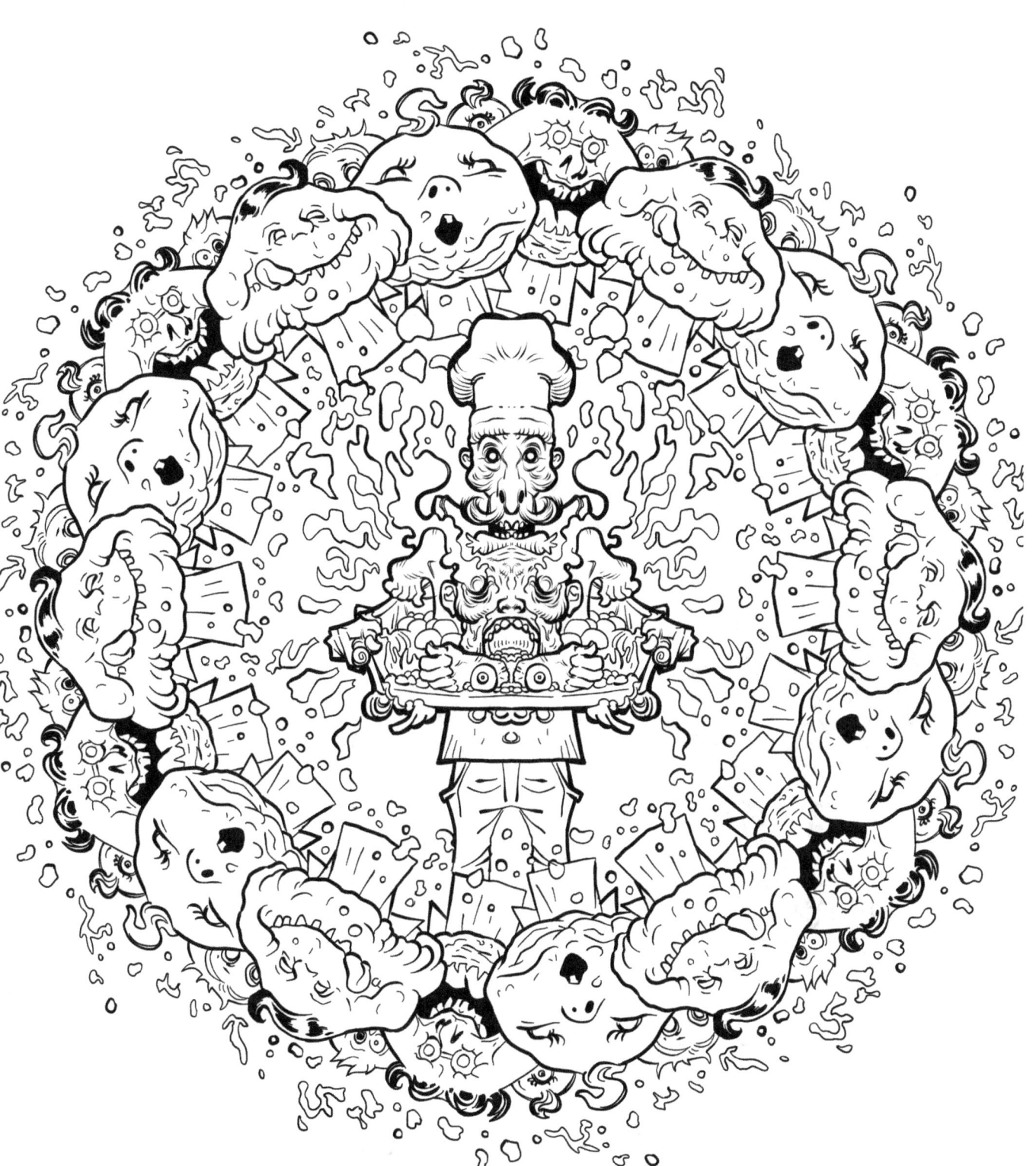

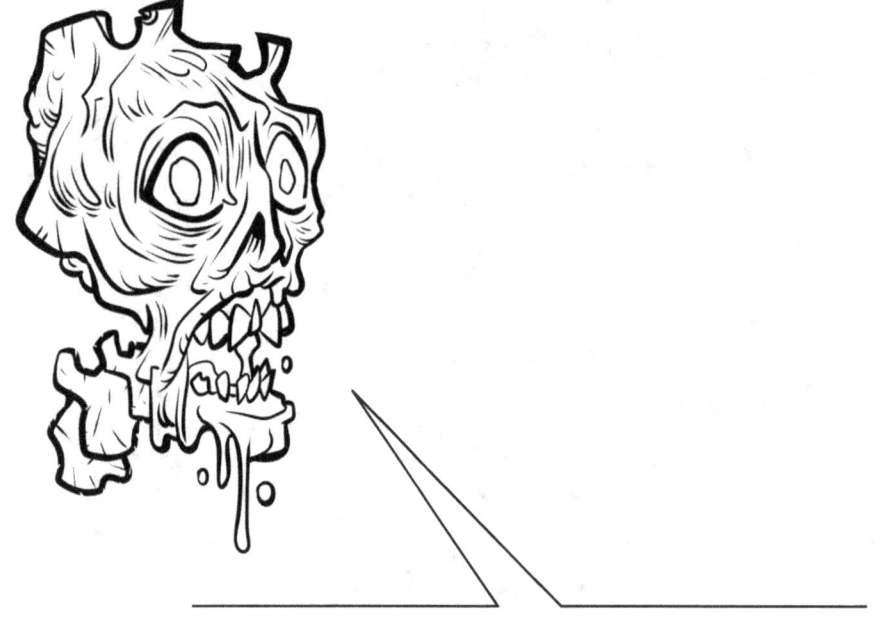

A CONTUMACIOUS CREATURE.

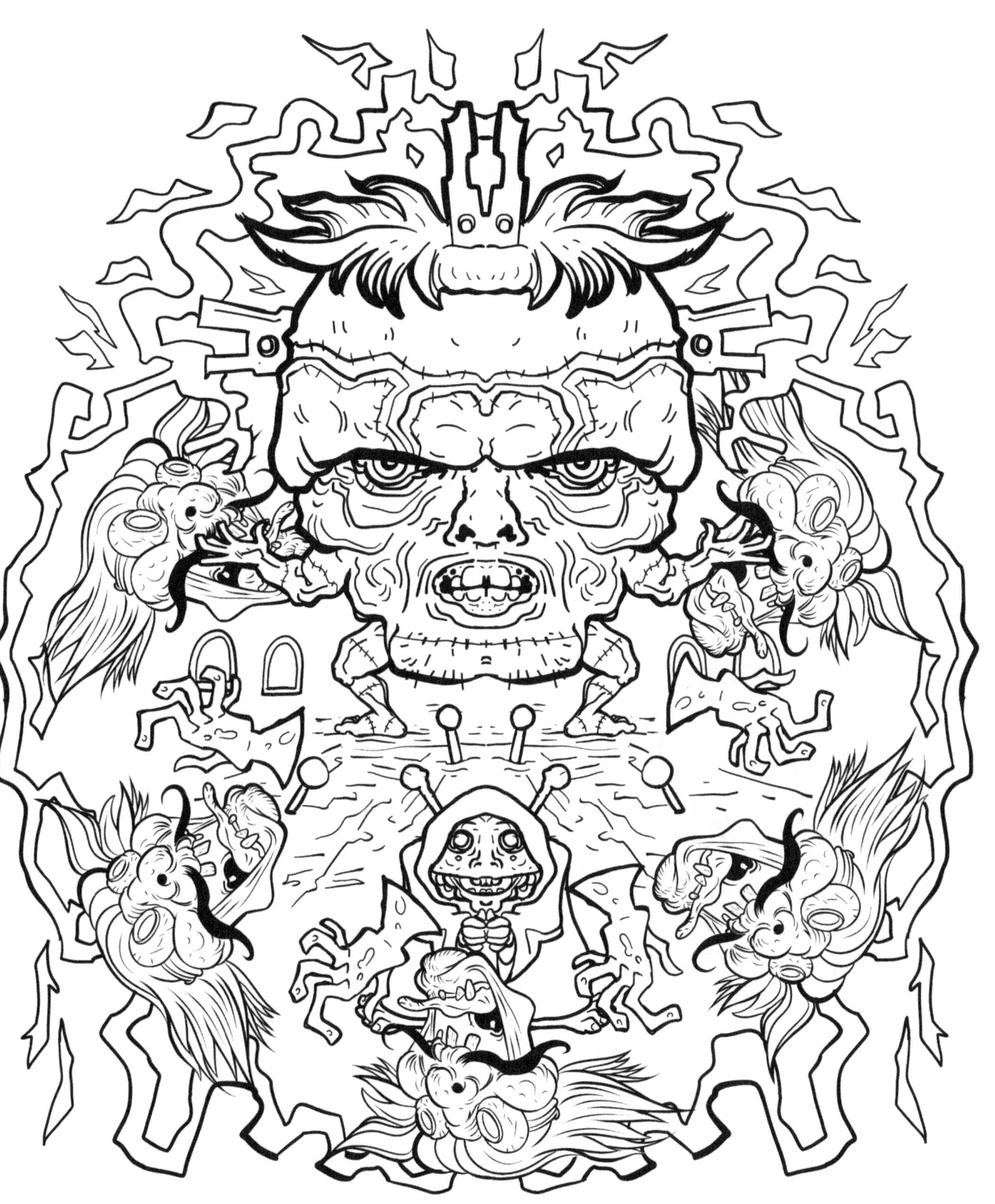

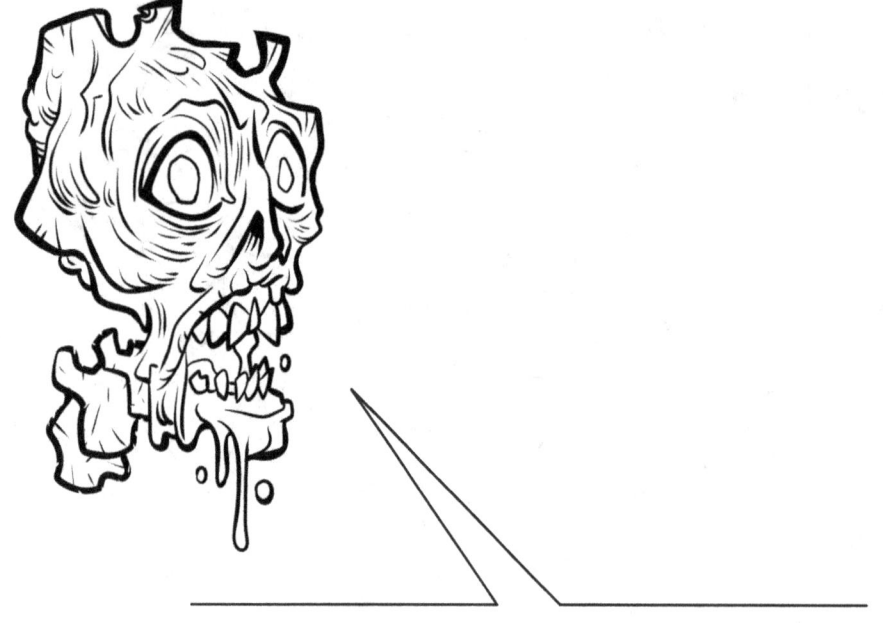

A SPECIAL GUEST.

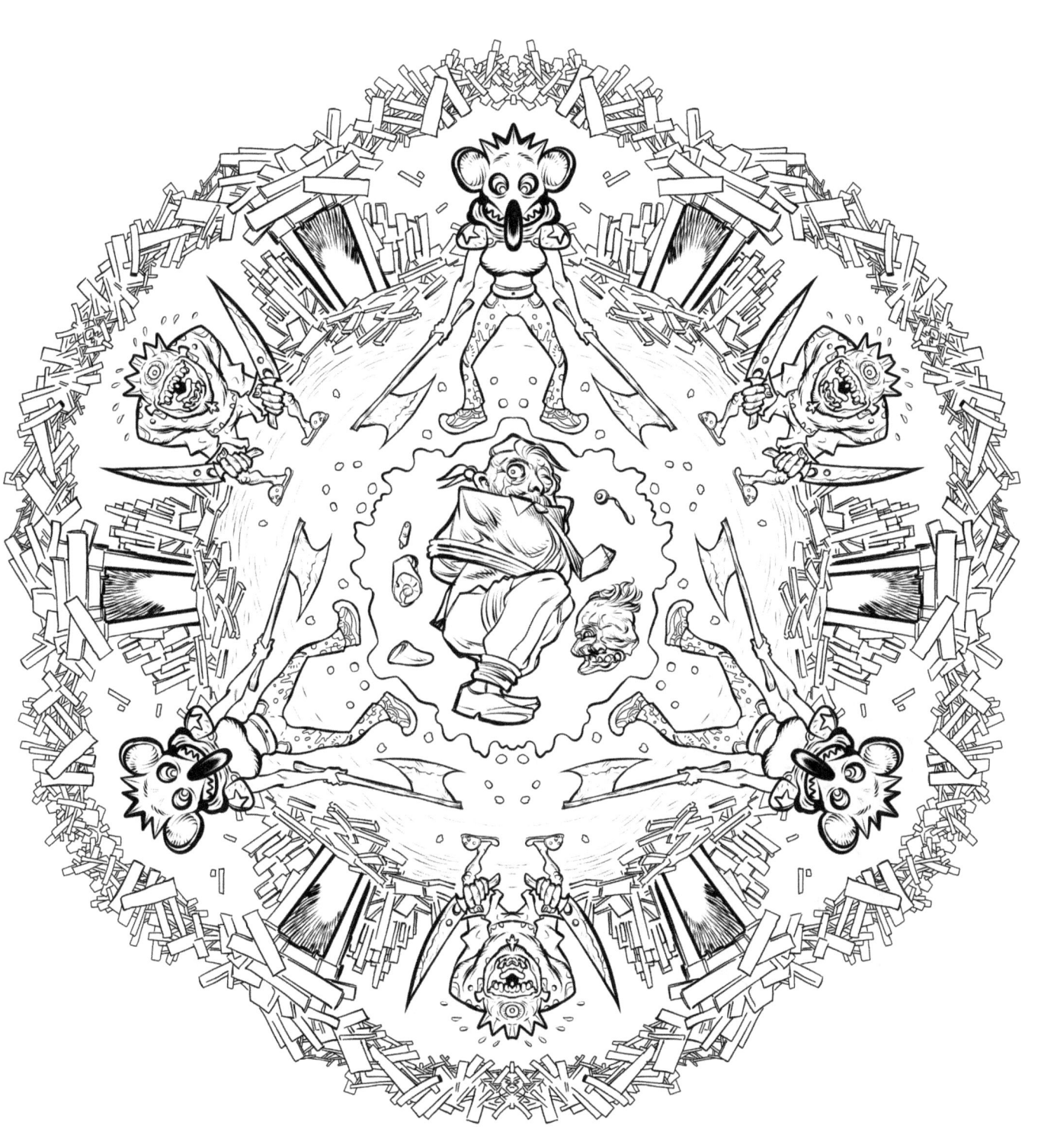

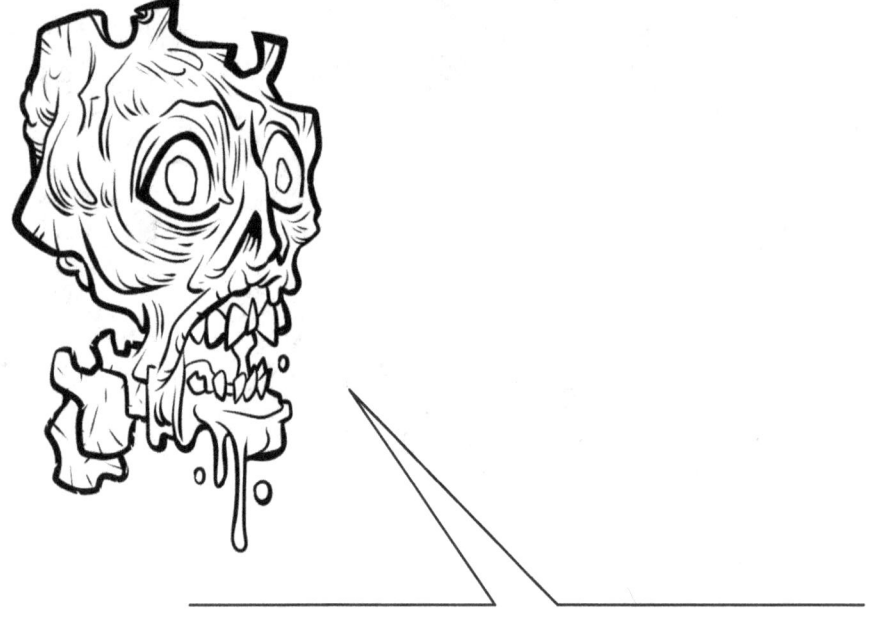

A RESTLESS MOON.

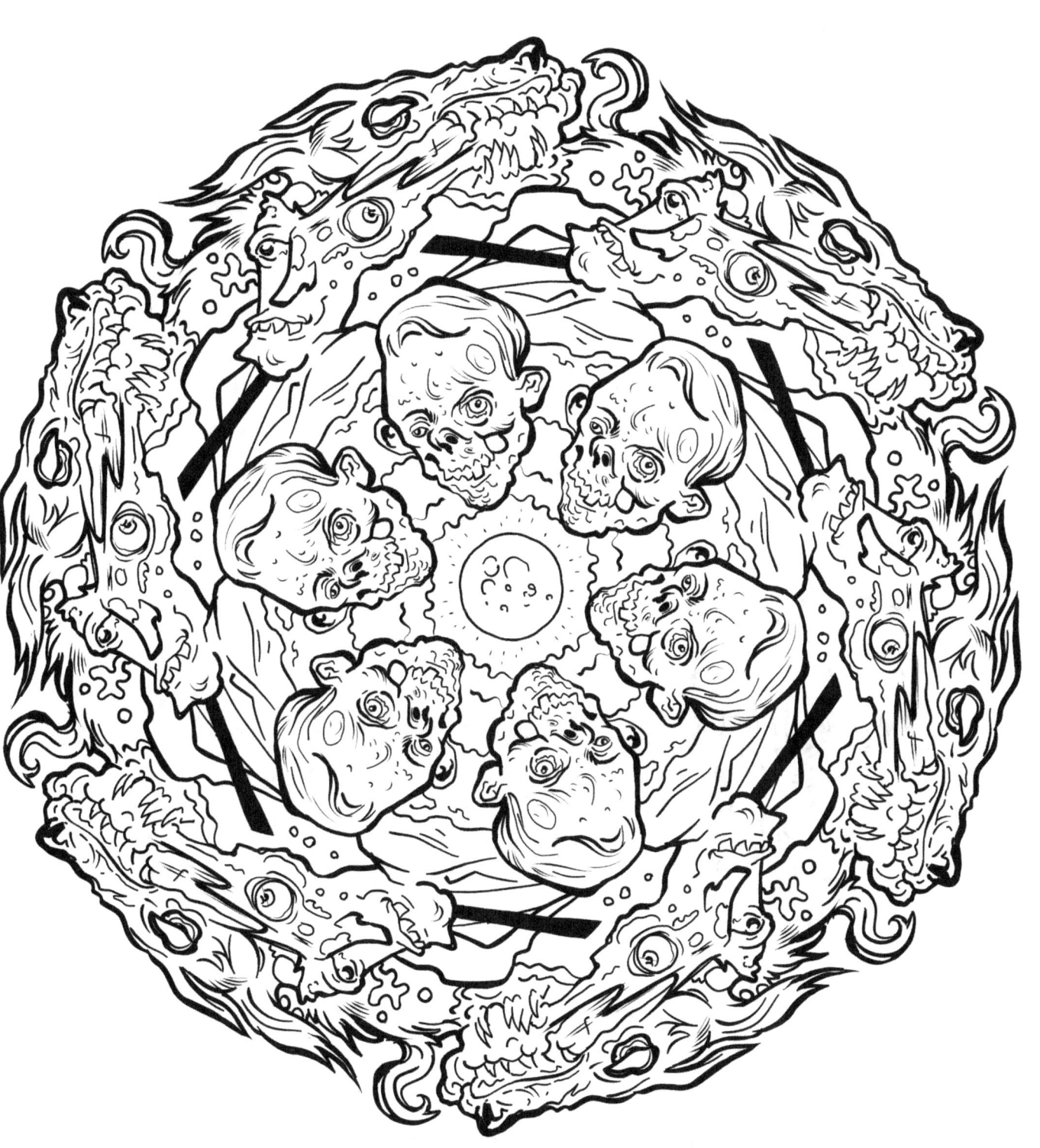

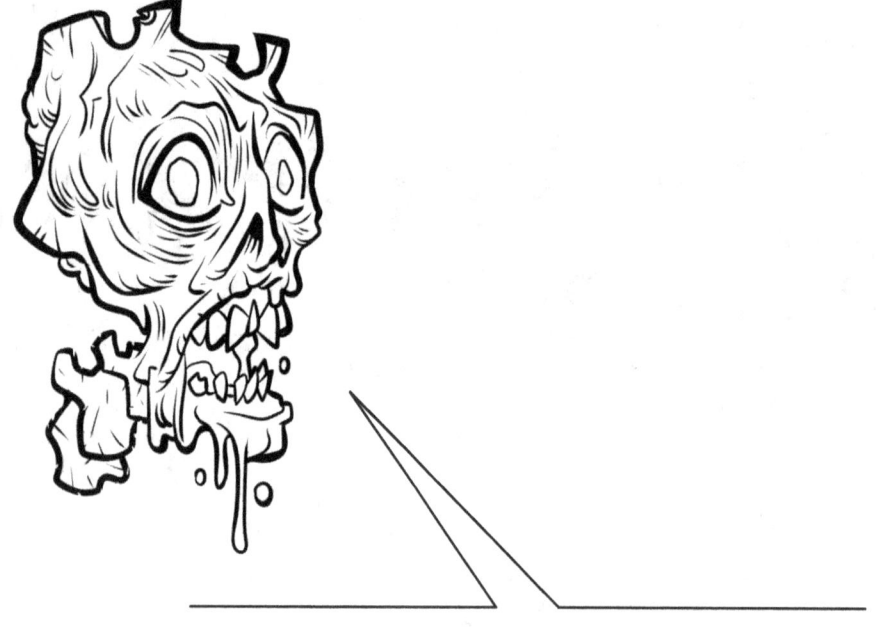

A NATURAL CHANT.

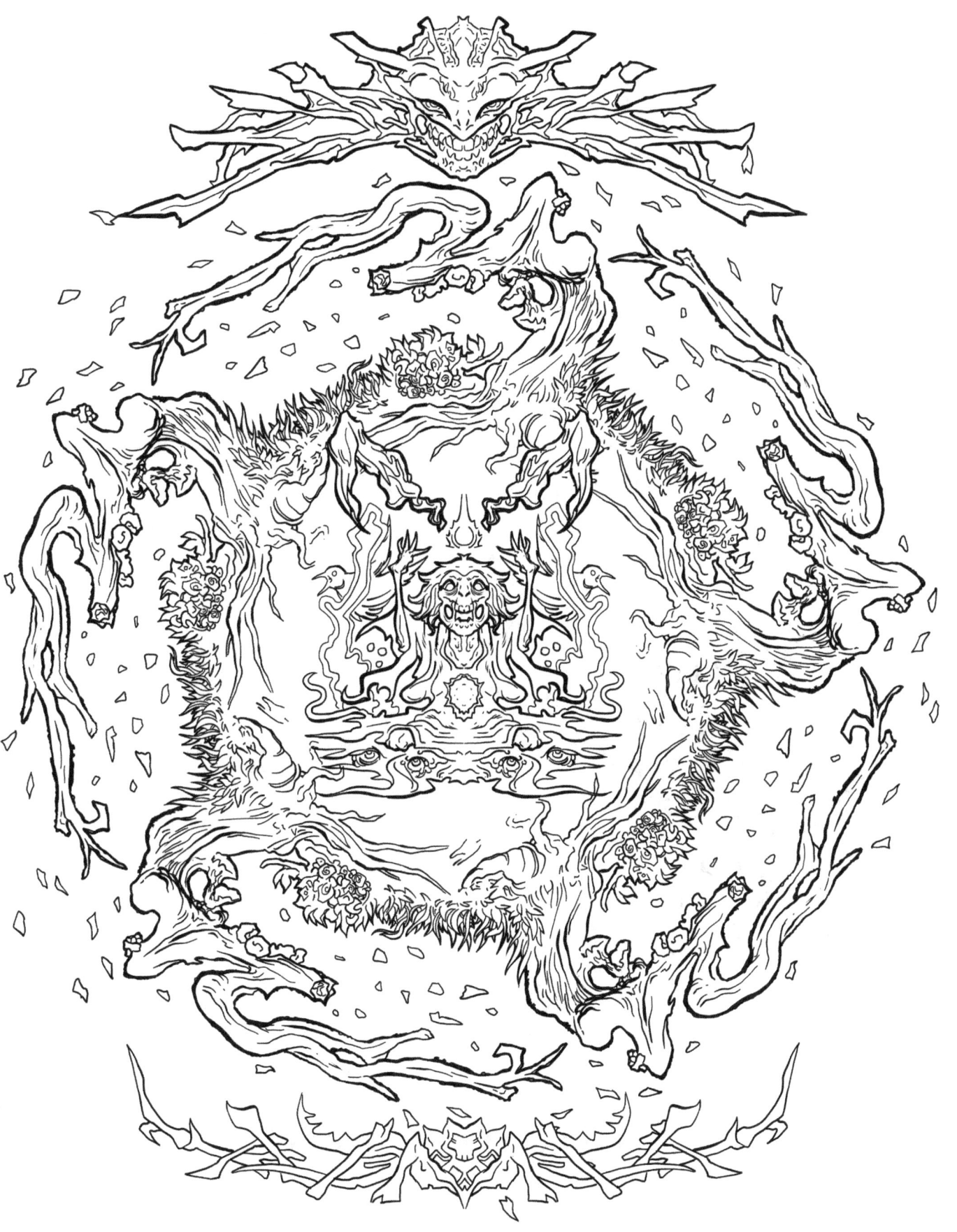

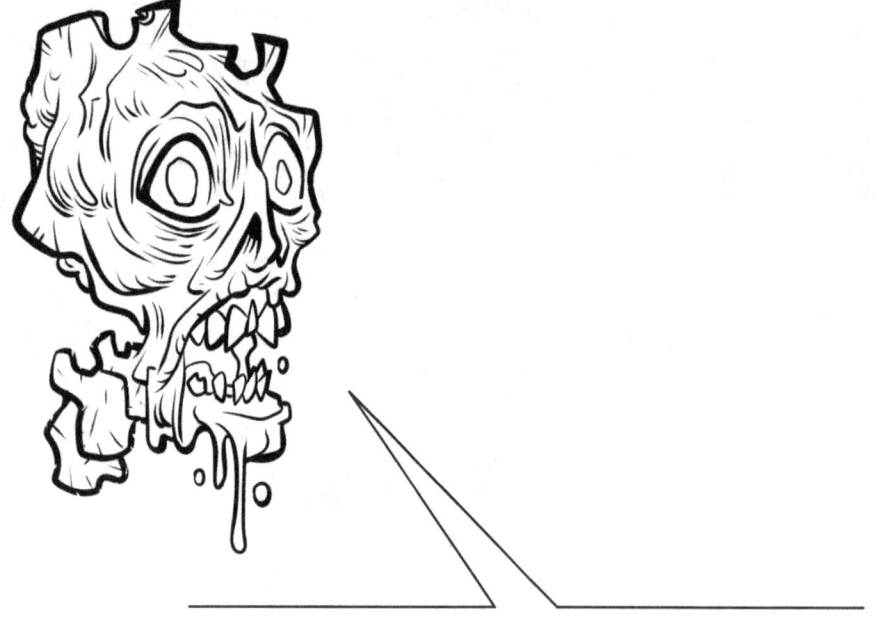

A DEVILISH TRIUMVIRATE.

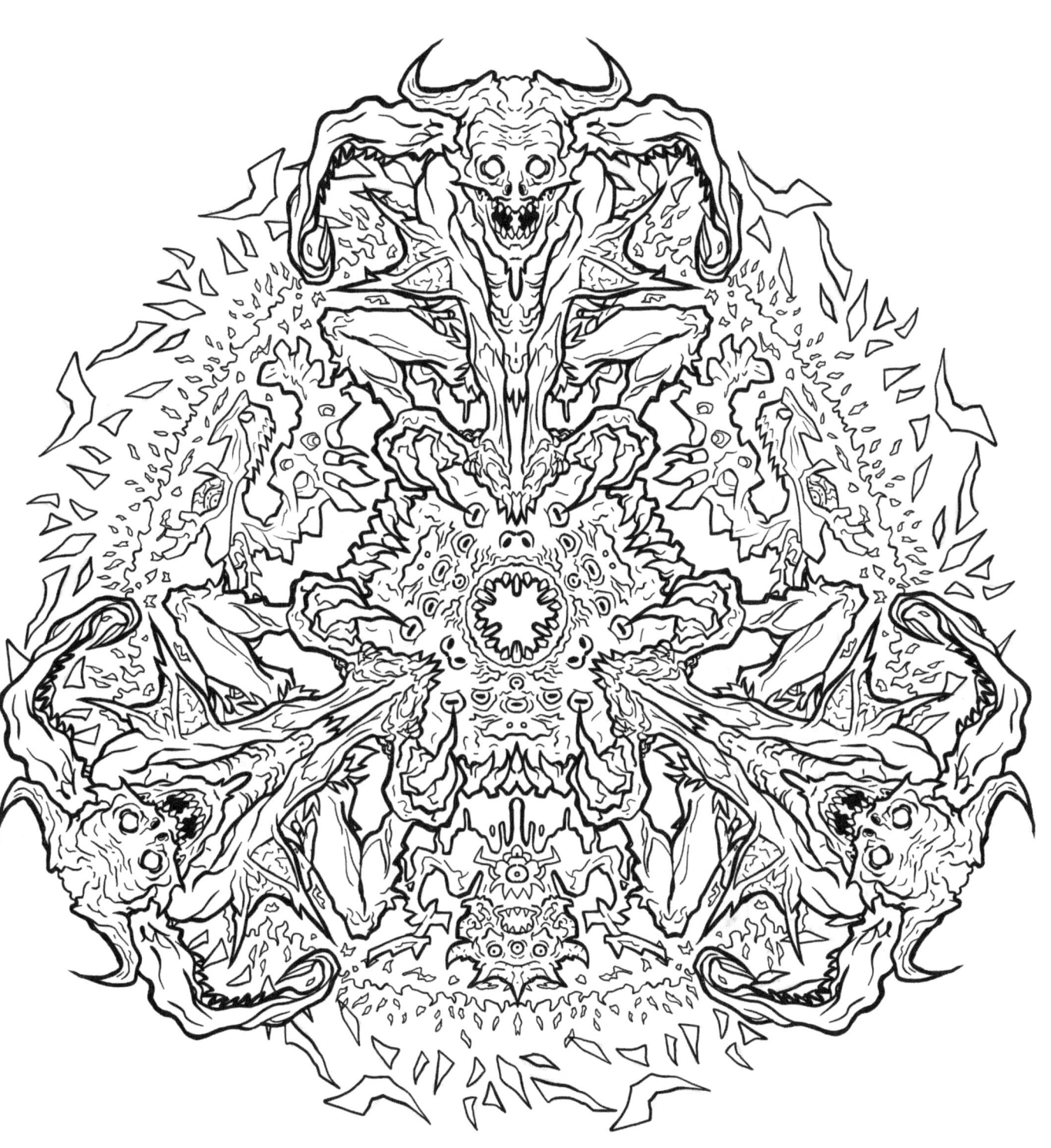

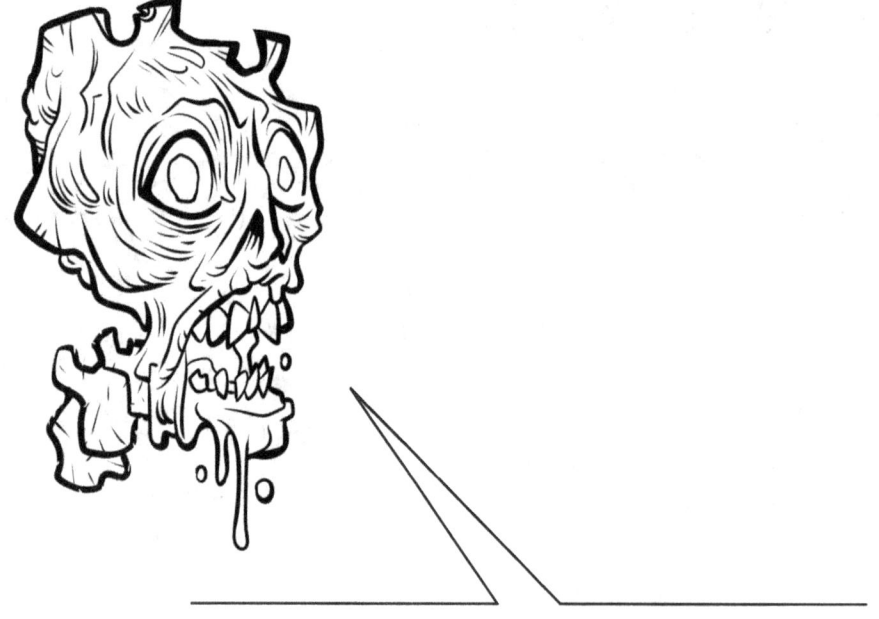

A SPLASHY SITUATION.

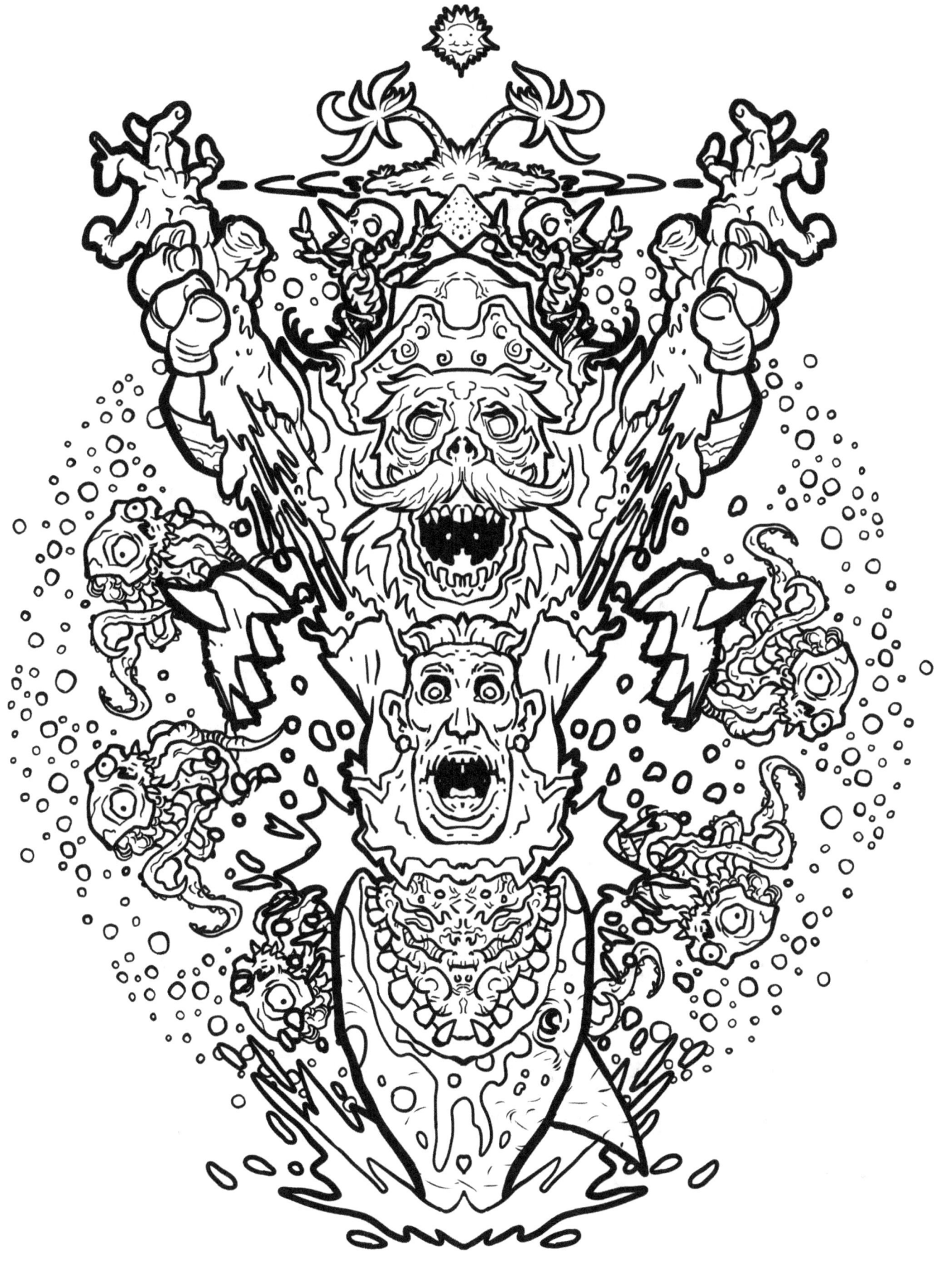

HORROR MANDALAS - A HORROR COLORING BOOK FOR ADULTS

VOL. 1

HORROR COLORING BOOKS BY SPOOKYDAYS

ILLUSTRATED BY DAVE YOUKOVICH

WWW.SPOOKYDAYS.COM

www.ingramcontent.com/pod-product-compliance
Lightning Source LLC
Chambersburg PA
CBHW060439220526
45465CB00008B/3197